DEATH OF A
STATESMAN

DEATH OF A STATESMAN

*The Solution to the
Murder of Olof Palme*

Ruth Freeman

ROBERT HALE · LONDON

© Focus Enterprises Ltd 1988
First published in Great Britain 1989

Robert Hale Limited
Clerkenwell House
Clerkenwell Green
London EC1R 0HT

British Library Cataloguing in Publication Data

Freeman, Ruth
Death of a statesman : the solution to the death
of Olof Palme
1. Sweden. Palme, Olof. Assassination
I. Title
364.1'524'0924

ISBN 0-7090-3698-1

Photoset in North Wales by
Derek Doyle & Associates, Mold, Clwyd.
Printed in Great Britain by
St Edmundsbury Press Ltd, Bury St Edmunds, Suffolk.
Bound by WBC Bookbinders Limited.

Contents

Illustrations

Illustrations

Preface

All the events described in this book actually happened, although the dialogue has been paraphrased. This is not one of those yarns where fiction is presented as truth. Quite the reverse: the facts are so fantastic that it is necessary to remind the reader that these things really occurred – Operation Cobra did attempt to extort £155 million, the Iraqi intelligence service did murder one of their agents who tried to defect, and hacked his body into fifty-seven pieces. And the Prime Minister of Sweden, the United Nations mediator in the Gulf War, was gunned down in one of the main streets of the capital.

The killer of Olof Palme walked away and has never been traced. The mere fact that no individual or organization has ever claimed credit for the killing, and the behaviour of the assassin, who carried out the act without uttering a word or even a cry, are sufficient evidence to discredit those theories which explained the murder as being motivated by revenge or political or social protest. And it was too efficiently executed to be the work of a casual killer or a madman.

In the distant past, the Chileans, the South Africans or the CIA might have been suspects, but at the time there was only one group who had both the means and a valid motive. So, in the words of Sherlock Holmes, 'When you have eliminated the impossible, whatever remains, *however improbable*, is the truth.'

In arriving at my conclusion, I have been able to use information which has never previously been published and in order to protect my sources, as well as myself, I have had recourse to three pseudonymous characters. Birger Trovald and Erik Johansson have suffered alterations to their personalities as well as to their names. The other disguised person is, of course, myself. Sven Beckman and a few minor characters have been invented, but the only other person to have been given a false name is the Iraqi agent, posing as a refugee: the interview and the police officer who interrogated him are real enough, but the name 'Omar Abdulkader' was invented rather than to indicate to the Iraqis which of their agents had been apprehended.

I would have liked to dedicate this book to those people who have helped me, but they must perforce remain unnamed.

Is this an outrageous story? Yes, but it is not the solution to the crime which is outrageous but the circumstances of the crime itself.

Ruth Freeman

1

Prelude to Two Murders

The setting sun over Baghdad dyed the wisps of cloud the colour of blood. Men and women were returning to their homes from shops and offices, the scattering of uniforms among the crowds a reminder of the war against Iran which dragged on interminably. Some of those men in drab battle-fatigues would be shedding their blood in the swampy marshes around the Shatt-el-Arab or on the scorched desert sands or the harsh, stony soil in the north. There was little gaiety in the great city: the military government and the Ba'ath Party, which was the same thing, imposed an iron discipline, imprisoning and torturing and eventually murdering all who were suspected of being less than wholehearted in their zeal for the party and for the war which was threatening to bleed the country to death and defeat. President Saddem Hussein demanded the total subjection of every man, woman and child, mental as well as physical.

But there was another war being waged no less relentlessly, a struggle which rarely hit the headlines, a war fought by unknown men in the shadows in every city where Iraqis who dared to speak out against the bestialities of the regime had taken refuge. Men in the shadows sought out the refugees and liquidated them. These vengeance killings were made possible by the maintenance of what is, according to certain Western intelligence sources, the most extensive espionage network in Europe.

There had already been the first skirmish between the Mukhabarat, Iraq's hidden army of secret agents, and SÄPO, the Swedish Security Police. Chief Detective Inspector Hans Melin was the officer in charge of the Aliens Department of the Stockholm Police District. Over his desk there passed all

applications for residence permits by foreigners – and also every
application for political asylum. His unit interrogated all
applicants and submitted recommendations to the Immigration
Board. Melin was under observation by SÄPO officers: he was
passing information on refugees to the Soviet Union, but he was
also playing a more sinister game. SÄPO followed a man from
the airport to Melin's flat on Sveavägen, forced their way inside
and caught Melin handing over secret documents on refugees to
his visitor, who had paid for them with a few thousand dollars.
The man was an Iraqi. Since he had a diplomatic visa, he was
merely expelled. Melin was sentenced to six years imprisonment. Two 'diplomats' at the Iraqi Embassy, Kamal Fanar and
Shariff Taka, were declared *persona non grata* and ordered out of
the country. That was back in 1978.

Now, in December 1984, another Iraqi was preparing to fly to
Stockholm, also with a diplomatic visa. Hussein Abad had
applied in writing to the Swedish Embassy in Baghdad as a
member of the Iraqi Ministry of Foreign Affairs, and the
diplomatic visa had been granted immediately, once his name
had been checked and had not shown up in the list of
undesirables who were *persona non grata*. At about the same
time, a very attractive young woman had visited the Swedish
Embassy. Her name was Jamila Mustafa El-Chafej and she was a
Lebanese citizen, or that was how she was described on the
passport which she presented. She requested a tourist visa and
was able to provide a satisfactory financial statement. Her
application was examined by an official at the embassy and
judged to be genuine, so the visa was granted. Once she arrived
in Stockholm, Jamila Mustafa El-Chafaj who now called herself
Fatima, moved into an apartment in the DOMUS student block.
The apartment had been rented for her in advance; the rental
agreement had been completed by the Iraqi Embassy.

What caused Fatima and Abad to descend upon the Swedish
capital was an article which had appeared in a leading
Stockholm newspaper, *Svenska Dagbladet*. The journalist had
interviewed an Iraqi, Majed Husain, who complained at the
incredible slowness of the Swedish bureaucracy. He had been
one of those men in the shadows, a captain in the Mukhabarat,
but he had been sickened by the cruelty of the regime and had
defected in 1983. He had claimed political asylum and, after
interrogation by the Stockholm police, his case came up before

the Immigration Board for a decision. More than a year passed: the Board remained inscrutable, and Majed Husain grew desperate and wrote his letter to the paper. It was only a few days after it appeared that both Abad and Fatima applied for their Swedish visas.

If Majed Husain had hoped that his letter would spur the Immigration Board into activity, he was disappointed. Christmas and the New Year passed and Majed Husain, without any close friends in the country, was a very lonely man. If only he had a girlfriend in Stockholm, life would have been more bearable.

Then, on 9 January 1985, his luck changed dramatically. As if by magic, a beautiful Arab girl appeared out of the blue. Her smile was warm and welcoming, and all his long-repressed emotions broke through. He chatted to her excitedly, while glancing lasciviously at her enticing long legs. She was actually staying in Stockholm, and he had never until now had the fortune to set eyes upon her.

'We really ought to get to know each other better,' urged the besotted Majed Husain.

'Well, if you have nothing better to do, why don't you come back with me to my place?' replied Fatima, with just a hint of maidenly coyness.

What could he possibly have to do that could take precedence over so beguiling an invitation! His lust was a raging furnace: he could not get through her front door quickly enough. And that was the last time Majed Husain was seen alive – or in one piece. The next day, both Husein Abad and the woman who was sometimes Jamila Mustafa El-Chafej flew out of Stockholm. Abad ceased to be a member of the Iraqi Ministry of Foreign Affairs and went back to his desk in the Mukhabarat.

It was not until 17 March that someone out walking stumbled on a sack in a wood near Grödinge, a suburb of Stockholm. Inside were parcels, each containing part of a dismembered corpse. Although the body had been hacked into fifty-seven chunks, the Forensic Department of the Medical-Legal Institute of the Karolinska Hospital and the Violent Crimes Department of the Stockholm Police Department identified it as that of Majed Husain within a few hours. Examination of the flat in DOMUS by SÄPO revealed bloodstains on the floor and carpet which matched the blood of the murdered man, and it was established that the body had been butchered in the flat.

Painstakingly, SÄPO pieced together the story and, with the aid of the records of the Swedish Embassy in Baghdad, collected evidence which they were able to assemble into an over-whelming case against the two agents, assisted by persons from the Iraqi Embassy in Stockholm.

On 4 December 1985, a warrant was issued for the arrest of Jamila Mustafa El-Chafej, who is now officially listed as wanted by Interpol. Since Abad enjoyed diplomatic immunity, no further action could be taken against him.

Thus was set in train a series of events which culminated in another murder – this time not of a pathetic, lonely refugee but of a world figure, the man chosen by the United Nations to mediate in the war between Iran and Iraq.

2

The Man in the Shadows

It was one of those clear nights, the stars brilliant in the cloudless sky, but bitterly cold. The snow had settled and now lay, packed hard and icy, on the pavement. The man who was standing in front of a darkened shop window had turned up his overcoat collar. He was used to a climate warmer than Stockholm's on this, the last day of February 1986.

It was getting on for midnight on a bleak Friday and, although Sveavägen is one of the city's main streets, the traffic had thinned out, but the man's gaze never wavered from the brightly lit lobby of the cinema on the other side of the road. The Grand Cinema was showing *The Brothers Mozart*, and the last performance would be ending any minute. He tightened his grip on the Smith & Wesson .357 revolver in his pocket. Not long now. He peered as a few people emerged from the cinema, then relaxed as they went on their way. He was waiting for one particular party, a group of four, two men and two women.

But would his prey walk towards him or go in the other direction? He ought to retrace his steps the way he had come, towards Hötorget as far as the Rådmansgatan subway station: that was the most direct way back to his flat in Västerlånggatan. Palme and his wife had left their home at 8.40 that evening, and the man might have lain in wait there, but Västerlånggatan is a narrow street in the old part of town, not an ideal spot for an ambush and subsequent getaway. If he went the other way, the man knew that it would mean biding his time for another opportunity, for the opening of a chink in the armour of security when, as had happened tonight, the bodyguards would have been dismissed.

Suddenly he tensed. There they were, standing on the pavement, chatting. They would not hang around for long: it was too cold. He was not quite close enough to hear their voices but he saw the women embrace and the older man hug his son as they said goodbye for what was to be the last time. Then the younger man and his girlfriend hurried off; his mother and father turned and started to walk towards Hötorget. It was going to work out just as he had hoped.

The man glanced around. The younger couple had turned a corner and were out of sight. The solitary watcher sidled out of the shadows and followed the older man and woman. Matching his pace to theirs, he resisted the urge to hurry. He had chosen his spot carefully, about 200 metres from the cinema. As they came up to where the narrow alley of Tunnelgatan opened out onto Sveavägen, he quickened his step until he was almost abreast of the man and woman, who were talking quietly, oblivious to his approach. There were perhaps half a dozen people walking in the street, and a solitary car moved towards them, but the man's gaze was fixed unwaveringly on his quarry.

Suddenly he leaped forward and turned to face them, gun in hand. Before the couple could react, he had pumped two bullets at point-blank range into his victim. He turned away: he had seen the way his shots had smashed home, and he knew that the job had been well done. In a matter of seconds, the man had turned into the quiet side-street. Tunnelgatan is a pedestrian street: no car could chase him up there, and no passer-by was likely to run after a man with a gun. He disappeared into the night.

The sound of the shots echoed in the frozen air. Men and women started to run towards the inert body on the pavement, and the woman, hunched over him. The man in the passing car heard the shot. He reached for his car telephone.

In the Stockholm Police Headquarters, Detective Inspector Kocí yawned. He was in charge of the Radio Centre that night and had enjoyed a quiet evening. Stockholm is normally a rather tranquil city, with far less violent crime than many capitals. And on a midwinter weekend, with many of the citizens out of town and the empty streets snow-cocooned, Kocí was looking forward to getting back to the comforting warmth of his own home. He glanced at the clock: it was 23.21. A message was coming through, and a policeman called out to him, 'A man has just been shot at the corner of Sveavägen and Tunnelgatan'.

Kocí frowned. Could it be true, or was this some damned hoaxer? His doubt was immediately resolved. A taxi-driver had also heard what sounded like several shots in the vicinity and had called on his radio. The taxi company switchboard phoned the police.

Meanwhile the assassin was still making his way along Tunnelgatan. He could continue up through the tunnel at the end of the street or climb the steps up the steep rock face at the entrance to the tunnel. There were four separate exits to Tunnelgatan, each of which gave onto a street where a car could be parked. He could not have known that, before he had even got to the end of the street, the police had already received the alarm and that the first of them was almost on the spot.

The patrol car was standing by the kerb in Kungsgatan, the policemen inside talking, a hiss of static from their radio and the purr of the heater in the background. A man walked over and tapped at the window.

'What is it?' asked Chief Inspector Gösta Söderström.

'Down there. I heard gunshots. In Sveavägen, about a couple of hundred metres from here.'

Söderström looked at the man. He appeared to be sober, not the sort to play some silly prank. He nodded and told his driver to make for the spot. The car had barely swung out into the street when Kocí's message came over the radio.

'A shooting has been reported at the junction of Sveavägen and Tunnelgatan. Investigate and report immediately.'

Söderström reached for the radio.

'I'm on my way. Your message timed at 23.23.'

Two minutes later the patrol car drew up beside the small huddle of people.

'What's been going on?' he demanded.

The people moved aside, and he saw the body, a pool of blood staining the darkened snow.

Someone called out: 'The man who shot him ran into Tunnelgatan. It happened less than five minutes ago. If you go after him now, you can catch him.'

Söderström raced back to the car and called Kocí.

'I think the guy is dead. The killer is escaping up Tunnelgatan. Send out a general alert; then get an ambulance here quickly, in case we can save him.'

He went back to the little knot of people, standing in silence around the body in the snow. Other cars would be on their way now to seal off the roads at the end of Tunnelgatan; Söderström would be kept busy, cordoning off the area, getting first statements from the witnesses and trying to obtain a coherent account of what had happened. Why the hell should some man get himself shot in the middle of Stockholm? There was no sign of a struggle, nor any attempt at robbery. The woman whom Söderström guessed was the wife of the victim stared up at him and cried out,

'I'm Lisbeth Palme. Can't you see? That's my husband lying there! Olof Palme, the Prime Minister!'

Chief Inspector Söderström gazed at her in disbelief. Then, as he turned to look more closely at the recumbent figure, a wave of panic overwhelmed him. The leader of the nation, a man whose importance exceeded that of the king himself, was lying at his feet, his life-blood ebbing away. He rushed back to the car and called up the Radio Centre.

'The Prime Minister has been gunned down,' he gasped.

There was a pause, then came the voice of the radio operator: 'Repeat your message.'

'Good God, I mean it! The Prime Minister has been shot.'

Kocí was aghast but he reacted swiftly. Two more patrol cars were raced to the spot to assist Söderström, and all cars were ordered to switch to another radio frequency immediately. But others had heard that first dramatic message.

What steps had, in fact, been taken to trap the murderer? When Kocí had received the first report from Söderström at the scene of the crime, he had at once ordered more cars to rush to the vicinity. But it was all very well telling the drivers to look out for a suspicious character: what he needed was a description. He called up Söderström.

'What's going on down there?' he asked.

'I've got both Olof and Lisbeth Palme off to a hospital, and I sent one of the cars after them to try to get a statement from Mrs Palme. Also I've managed to put some ropes around the spot until the guys from the Technical Branch get here.'

'Never mind that,' snapped Kocí. 'Have you got any sort of description from the witnesses?'

'They are as vague as hell,' Söderström complained bitterly.

'There are eight of them, and they don't agree on anything, except that it was definitely a man. Most of them have the impression that he was dark. And that's just about it.'

'A fat lot of use that is,' commented Kocí. 'What about the dogs?'

One of the first things he had done was to order that a pack of police dogs be rushed to the scene of the crime.

'They're here but they don't seem to be doing anything. Wait a moment while I check with their handler.'

Less than a minute later, Söderström was back on the air.

'Hopeless,' he reported. 'The guy says there have been so many people trampling around the place that the trail is too confused for the hounds. They're on their way back now.'

Kocí swore. 'We'll just have to hope that someone in one of the squad cars happens to notice some man behaving suspiciously. You stay there and liaise with the Violent Crimes and Technical teams when they arrive.'

Kocí had other things to do. Members of the Government had to be informed. A routine had been devised for dealing with just such an emergency. He consulted the printed instructions and ordered the telephone operator to put him through to Ulf Dahlsten, who, as Secretary to the Council of Ministers, would be responsible for assembling the members of the Government.

'What's his number?' asked the operator.

'How the hell do I know?' exploded Kocí.

'Shouldn't it be given in your instructions?'

'If it were, I would have told you. Some idiot must have forgotten to put it in. Look it up in the directory. And, for Christ's sake, hurry!'

Kocí waited in a frenzy of impatience. Minutes ticked by. Then the operator came on the line.

'Inspector, Dahlsten isn't listed in the directory. What do you want me to do?'

Kocí clenched his fists in impotent rage. There he was, in the hot seat, in the worst crisis to have hit Sweden for more than 200 years when Gustav III was murdered in 1782. With all the fantastic electronic paraphernalia at his disposal, he was unable even to pass on the information 'through the approved channels'.

'Look, there must be someone who has Dahlsten's number!' he shouted.

'What about calling the Government Office? There has to be someone on duty at the Chancery,' suggested the operator.

'Get on to them.'

Again Kocí waited. He glanced at the clock. Every move of the second-hand meant one more step by the killer away from his pursuers. Or perhaps towards some other minister, another target. Maybe the entire cabinet was in danger, and he could not get the warning out to them. He snatched up the phone.

'Haven't you been able to get that number yet?'

'Yes, Inspector. One of the security guards in the Chancery found it for me. But I can't get through. The line is busy: Dahlsten's talking to someone.'

Kocí groaned. It was a nightmare. 'Keep trying,' he ordered.

In fact, Dahlsten had decided to have an early night and was sound asleep when some time around midnight he was disturbed by the ringing of his phone. Still not fully awake, he fumbled for the phone in the dark.

'Hello. Who's there?' he demanded.

'Is that Ulf Dahlsten?'

'Yes. Who are you?' Dahlsten repeated. 'And what do you want, calling at this hour?'

'This is Kjell Lindström.'

'Who?' Dahlsten was not yet fully awake.

'Lindström, the Press Secretary to the Council of Ministers. Mr Dahlsten, I've heard that Olof Palme has been shot and killed.'

His words shattered the web of sleep: Dahlsten sat bolt upright in bed.

'What do you mean, Lindström, "you've heard"? Have you spoken with the police, with SÄPO?'

'Yes, but they know nothing, or at least that's what they say. It's like this. I was called by a journalist who said he'd heard something on the police radio network. You know a lot of these people tune in to the police frequency to pick up scraps of news. Well, I first thought the guy might be playing a particularly morbid practical joke on me, but just to make sure I called a security man who had been on duty as one of Palme's bodyguards that evening. He told me Palme had dismissed his guards for the night, and everything had been normal when he left. I guessed he would have heard if there had been an attempt on the Prime Minister's life later, but he offered to check with

SÄPO and call me back. A few minutes later he rang again and told me that SÄPO knew nothing about any shooting. But no sooner had I put down the phone than I got a call from another journalist, a man I know and trust, repeating the same story. I told him I'd checked with SÄPO, but then two more journalists were on the phone to me within a few minutes. Well, by that time I reckoned there must be something in the story, and that's why I've got on to you.'

'All right, all right,' Dahlsten interrupted. 'It's probably some sort of misunderstanding, but you were right to let me know. I'll check again.'

Dahlsten hung up and thought for a moment. The security man probably did not know which department of SÄPO would have up-to-the-minute information. Dahlsten called the duty officer at the twenty-four-hour Emergency Office.

'We have nothing here,' replied the officer. 'How long ago was this police message supposed to have gone out?'

'The journalist told Lindström it was about half past eleven.'

'That's forty minutes ago. If there had been any incident, we ought to have had it in here by now, but I'll get through to the Radio Centre of the Stockholm Police District and find out if they can cast any light on it. Hold on.'

The SÄPO duty officer was connected to Inspector Kocí, who was still vainly trying to contact Dahlsten.

'*Satan!*' shouted Kocí. 'Here I am with an urgent message for Dahlsten, and his phone is constantly occupied. Now I find he's chattering away to you. Please, tell him to hang up immediately.'

So it was that Dahlsten was eventually officially informed of the death of the Prime Minister by Kocí, about three-quarters of an hour after it was known by a handful of journalists – and anyone else who had listened to the police radio and had picked up Söderström's anguished report.

But what about SÄPO, the Security Police? The duty officer, having passed on Kocí's request to Dahlsten to hang up, realized that, although he had not received any report in his office, something serious must have occurred, and on his own initiative called his superintendent, Alf Karlsson.

'It sounds as if Olof Palme has been assassinated and the Stockholm Police are dealing with it,' said the duty officer.

Karlsson acted decisively. 'I'm on my way,' he said. 'Try and get whatever information is available.'

He called up one of his detective inspectors to come on duty with him, and sent a car racing round to Palme's flat, where he had a guard mounted by quarter past midnight. A few minutes later, Karlsson strode into his office.

'All right,' he growled at the duty officer. 'Let's have it. What have you found out?'

The man was tense. 'It's true. One of the police patrol cars was on the spot almost at once. Shouldn't we take over?'

Karlsson did not waste time answering. He grabbed a phone and called the head of SÄPO, Sven-Åke Hjälmroth.

'Maybe it's only a remote chance, but suppose there *is* some terrorist group acting to destroy the Government. Ought we not to take measures to protect the other ministers?'

'I'll deal with that,' replied Hjälmroth. 'Get someone over to Palme's apartment.'

'I've sent a car. They should be there by now.' Karlsson glanced at his watch. It was seventeen minutes past midnight. 'I'll get a team of the boys from our Technical Department over there to check if the place has been bugged. If a foreign espionage service is responsible, they would probably have kept the place under surveillance, and we ought to be able to find some trace.'

'Get on with it!' ordered Hjälmroth, and hung up.

More and more SÄPO personnel reported for duty, and soon the office was buzzing with activity. Karlsson was pleased to see among the first arrivals Per-Göran Näss, head of counter-espionage, immaculately dressed as always in a dark suit of conservative cut, as though it were everyday procedure for him to be called out of bed in the middle of the night, and Sture Höglund, chief of the bodyguard section, both of whom had been awakened by Hjälmroth.

While the Security Police were fully occupied, with Höglund setting bodyguards to protect ministers, and Näss mobilizing his staff to search for any signs of unusual activity by a foreign intelligence service or an international terrorist organization, the regular members of the Stockholm Police District of the national force were following up the actual investigation of the murder and the trail of the killer. Before Söderström had finished roping off the scene of the crime and rounding up the witnesses, Kocí had sent a patrol car to pick up Superintendent Sune Sandström.

Then the unfortunate Kocí hit another snag. It was vital to get hold of Hans Holmér, the head of the Stockholm Police District, since he was the man responsible for investigating all crimes committed within the city limits, and not even SÄPO itself was authorized to interfere unless it could be shown to be a matter of state security. No one was yet in a position to establish whether the murder of Olof Palme was a political crime and whether state security was involved. So it was essential to bring in Hans Holmér. At least they knew Holmér's number, but Stockholm's police chief had gone away for the weekend.

'Where can we find him?' demanded Kocí.

'I heard that he has taken off for somewhere in Dalarna for a couple of days' skiing,' called one of the officers.

'By car?' asked Kocí.

'I guess so.'

'He could be anywhere,' Kocí snorted. 'Send out a general alert to every police station from here to Dalarna and let me know the moment he's been located.'

Meanwhile Kocí was able to lay his hands on Holmér's deputy, Gösta Welander, and another squad car was despatched to bring him to headquarters. Kocí was worried. He had played it according to the book, but he fervently prayed that Holmér would be found quickly. The city's chief policeman was very jealous of his position and acutely conscious that his appointment, by Olof Palme himself, had not been popular with many of the professional police, who regarded him as a mere political appointee. They could not delay taking action until the missing chief was found, but Kocí was sure that Holmér would resent any intimation that the case was being taken out of his hands.

Also, before midnight, Chief Detective Inspector Nils Linder, responsible for the Violent Crimes Division, was on his way to the headquarters, and more and more subordinate officers were ordered to report for duty. Shortly after a quarter past midnight, Söderström checked in with the eight witnesses. Linder, learning that the witnesses were unable to give a coherent description of the assassin, ordered a couple of officers from the Violent Crimes Division to drive to the Sabbatsbergs Hospital and obtain an account from Lisbeth Palme.

'I've already sent a patrol car there,' Söderström pointed out.

'And I sent another couple of my men as well,' said Kocí.

'This is a matter which needs handling by my division,' replied Linder. 'Get me Lange,' he told the switchboard.

Chief Detective Inspector Vincent Lange was the head of the Stockholm Police District's Technical Department. Linder told him briefly what had happened.

'Get over to Sveavägen with some of your men. See if you can find spent bullets or anything else which might be useful. You never know, the man might even have thrown the gun away. But hurry, before there are too many people there, getting in the way and destroying whatever evidence there is.'

Meanwhile Kocí frantically checked with the patrol cars which were scouring the streets of Stockholm but, as the minutes passed without any news, the scent grew fainter and he sensed that the hunted man was slipping ever deeper into the darkness of the night. And while departmental chiefs in both the Security Police and the Stockholm Police District on different floors of the same building sent out their own frantic orders, often overlapping, the overall boss, Hans Holmér, who should have been co-ordinating and controlling the operation, had apparently vanished into thin air as completely as the assassin himself.

When he had first arrived on the spot, Söderström had taken charge in the street and waited impatiently for other officers to arrive. He looked down helplessly at the shattered body of the Prime Minister. Sporadic traffic was passing, and it happened that one of the first vehicles was an ambulance. It was not from one of the Stockholm hospitals but Söderström ran into the road, waving his arms. The ambulance screeched to a halt. A minute later, with Olof and Lisbeth Palme inside, it was tearing down the street with siren blaring and lamp flashing. It was less than a kilometre to the Sabbatsbergs Hospital and, warned by the police by radio, the staff were prepared for an emergency. The moment the ambulance came to a halt, the doors were wrenched open and the stretcher on which Palme's body had been placed was rushed inside. Barely ten minutes had elapsed since Olof Palme had been shot.

The duty doctor, Claes Wallin, needed little more than a glance to realize the gravity of the case. The Prime Minister was still alive, but one of the bullets had severed the aorta. He was unconscious and had lost a great deal of blood. Wallin did everything in his power to staunch the flow, and while he was still engaged in the desperate battle to save Palme's life, the first police car arrived, sent by Söderström. Two inspectors, Dahlsgaard and Christiansson, bustled in.

'Can he talk?' asked one of the young police officers.

Neither Wallin nor Lisbeth Palme could be bothered to answer. It was obvious to everyone that Olof Palme would never utter another word in this world. Almost at once, another car, sent this time by Kocí from the twenty-four-hour emergency unit, drew up and two more police officers, Rimborn and Torstensson, joined the others. While the doctor and the nurses carried on their futile struggle to save the fatally wounded man, the police officers decided how to deal with their situation.

Inspectors Rimborn and Christiansson approached Lisbeth Palme.

'We are deeply sorry,' said Rimborn, 'and you know that the police will do everything possible to bring the killer to justice. We won't detain you for long, but please tell us what you can.'

'It was over so quickly. I hardly saw anything.'

'But at any rate you must have caught a glimpse of the man. It was a man, wasn't it?'

Lisbeth nodded. 'I'm sure it was a man.'

'Anyone you knew?' pressed Christiansson.

Lisbeth hesitated. 'He seemed somehow familiar, but it was not anyone I recognized. Maybe I've seen him hanging around in the street.'

'Please, do try,' urged Rimborn. 'It's important.'

She shook her head impatiently. 'Do you think I don't realize that? But I tell you, I can't remember. He was dark. I might have seen him in a film or in a newspaper or magazine. I honestly don't know.'

One of the nurses came out of the operating theatre. She looked anxiously at Lisbeth Palme and cried out, 'But, Mrs Palme, you are wounded!'

Lisbeth gazed at her in bewilderment. The nurse pointed to a hole in her fur coat. Lisbeth felt the spot and realized for the first time that she too had been hit. The nurse helped her take off the heavy coat, but they both turned as Dr Wallin walked out of the operating theatre towards them. He looked at Lisbeth Palme and shook his head.

'I'm sorry,' he said.

The nurse called out to him, 'Dr Wallin, can't you see? Mrs Palme has been wounded too.'

It took only a few minutes. The thickness of her coat had been something of a protection, and the bullet had merely grazed her skin. Dr Wallin asked the nurse to put a plaster on the scratch.

'Please think if there isn't anything more definite you can remember,' Rimborn persisted.

Something seemed to snap inside her. 'I've told you, I don't know anything more,' she cried. 'Now please leave me alone. There's nothing more I can tell you.'

While this exchange was taking place, the body of Olof Palme had been moved into another room, and Inspector Torstensson had mounted guard over it.

They had been in the hospital less than half an hour when Wallin signed the death certificate. The news was spreading, and more and more people arrived at Sabbatsbergs Hospital. Lisbeth Palme was sitting in one of the offices and waiting – for what? Ministers, colleagues of her late husband, came and paid their respects. The shocked woman listened but said nothing: what was there to say? Time passed. There was a tiny ray of consolation with the arrival of her sons. The young men did what they could to comfort their mother. There was a gentle tap on the door, and a nurse looked in.

'I'm sorry to disturb you, Mrs Palme, but there are more detectives, this time from the Violent Crimes Division, and they have asked to have a few words with you.'

Lisbeth Palme called out to the two detectives, waiting behind the nurse.

'Go away. I've told the others all I know. I have nothing more to say, so please, for God's sake, leave me in peace.'

Mårten put his arm around his mother and gestured to the policemen to go.

'We do have some urgent questions,' protested one of them.

'There's nothing I can add to what I've already said,' Lisbeth Palme repeated impatiently.

'But he was the Prime Minister.'

'He was my husband. Leave me alone.'

'Will you allow us to take your fur coat for forensic examination?' demanded one of the detectives.

'Good God, there's just a hole in it, that's all,' cried the bereaved woman. 'Haven't I suffered enough tonight without having to put up with stupid red tape? Leave the coat here and go away.'

The nurse pushed the men out of the way and went out, closing the door behind her.

'Unco-operative, that's what she is,' grumbled one of the disappointed policemen. 'How are we supposed to catch the swine who did this if we can't even get a proper statement from his wife who was holding his arm when he was shot.'

'But Mrs Palme has made a statement,' pointed out the nurse, as the two detectives started to walk away.

'Not to us, and it's the Violent Crimes Division who have to deal with this, not some crude cops from Traffic Control or a passing patrol car or anyone else who just happens to be on the spot at the time,' replied the first detective.

'She's got no consideration,' the second detective added.

'Hadn't you better get on with finding the murderer, instead of wasting your time pestering the poor woman?' blazed the nurse.

Back in the office, Mrs Palme turned to her sons.

'Take me home, please,' she asked.

But Mårten shook his head. 'Not yet. We have to wait a little longer,' he told her. 'The Security Police are in the apartment, checking.'

'SÄPO! What are they after?'

Mårten shrugged his shoulders. 'Looking to see if the place has been bugged, I suppose. They've promised to phone here when it's clear.'

The detectives from the Violent Crimes Division, foiled in their attempt to take away Lisbeth's fur coat, talked for a while with Dr Wallin. Then they arranged for the corpse of Olof Palme to be removed to the Legal Institute of the Karolinska Hospital, a few kilometres away, for further examination.

It was not until three in the morning that Lisbeth Palme and her sons arrived back in her home with a heavy police escort. That was 6½ hours after she had left the flat with her husband for a quiet evening at the cinema, and 3½ hours since Olof Palme had been murdered. The family waited to hear news of the capture of the assassin, and, by then, so did the whole of Sweden.

*

At ten minutes to two, the three SÄPO chiefs, Hjälmroth, Näss and Höglund, strode into the police headquarters. They found Kocí still vainly trying to make contact with Holmér.

'We can't wait for him,' snapped Hjälmroth. 'We need whatever information you've managed to get and plan our next moves. Is Welander here?' Kocí nodded. 'Well, that's all right then. There's a valid representative of the Stockholm Police District. You get your crew from the National Police together. We have enough to do putting security guards on ministers and all other potential targets. And I suppose we had better pass the news to the King.'

As he spoke, Welander hurried in. He cocked his head enquiringly at Hjälmroth.

'So what do you think in SÄPO? Is it likely that agents of a foreign country have carried out this murder?'

Hjälmroth turned to Näss. 'Well?'

Näss, a chubby-faced man in his mid forties, puffed at one of those oversized cigars which he seemed to smoke incessantly. Even in the depths of the crisis, he maintained his calm, and the good-humoured twinkle never left his eyes. However, he chose his words with care, before replying in his light, Wärmland accent.

'As I am sure you are aware, it is not the policy of SÄPO, or any other national intelligence agency, to disclose its actions to unauthorized persons. However, I can tell you that, before coming here, I alerted several specialists whose duties include keeping a watchful eye on certain foreign embassies and consulates as well as on individuals whom we believe to be connected with terrorist groups. Sweden has had its differences with a number of countries, and I am sure there are people in both the CIA and the KGB who were opposed to Palme and to some of the specific policies he followed, but I cannot believe that any of these points of friction were of such gravity as to lead them to an action of such a drastic nature. Of course, we shall continue to look into every possibility, but, as of now, I have nothing at all positive for you.'

'But it's still possible that some intelligence agency or terrorist organization is involved, and it's the responsibility of SÄPO to ensure the safety of the rest of the Government,' Welander observed. 'Stockholm Police District has enough to do organizing the whole complex operation of detecting the criminal; your people must look after security.'

Hjälmroth turned to him.

'I'm going to the Chancery building to make sure that the quorum of ministers and the building itself are adequately protected. As you have pointed out, Mr Welander, it's the job of the Stockholm Police District to hunt down the criminal. We'll leave you to get on with it.'

With an unfriendly nod in the direction of Welander, Hjälmroth walked out, followed by Näss and Höglund. Sandström, who had come into Kocí's office, watched them go and frowned. The rivalry between the regular police and the Security Police and the very special status of the Stockholm Police District were not going to make the capture of the assassin any easier.

Hjälmroth drove to the Chancery, the nerve-centre of the Swedish Government, where he found the door guarded by a solitary policeman and that the necessary quorum of five ministers had all arrived by taxi without waiting for any bodyguards. Hjälmroth was furious and ordered that the guard on the building be increased. Back in the offices of SÄPO, he ordered Höglund to ensure that the ministers' bodyguards were on the spot. The men from the Security Police then concentrated on spreading their protection over the key men in the political life of Sweden.

Communicating with the King proved to be more problematic than they had anticipated. First, they had to find out in which of his half-dozen palaces or official residences His Majesty was spending the weekend. That was easy, since a couple of SÄPO guards had been sent to watch over him. As luck would have it, the King and the SÄPO men had left Stockholm for the country, and the royal party were staying in the skiing lodge at Storlien, about 600 kilometres north-west of the capital. Hjälmroth phoned the rural retreat, but no one answered. The King had retired for the night long ago, and his equerry was lodged in a part of the building too far away for him to be able to hear the phone, as was the solitary sentry stationed outside. As for the security guards, they were not even in the building, having been sent off for the night to a nearby hotel. But which hotel, and what was its number? (It was the Storliens Högfjällshotel, with a splendid view over the mountains.)

It was not until nearly five-thirty in the morning that the King of Sweden was awakened to be informed of the murder of his prime minister. However, as one of the SÄPO bosses remarked, what did it matter, since the King has absolutely no constitutional powers and passing on the news to him was no more than an act of courtesy?

Other people were more relevant.

'Have you allocated bodyguards to everyone, Höglund?' asked Hjälmroth.

'Everyone except Ingemund Bengtsson.'

'Good God, man, as the Speaker of the Parliament, he's vital. No new Government can be installed without him,' exclaimed Hjälmroth.

'He's on holiday in Spain,' Höglund explained. 'He has an apartment in Málaga, and we believe he's there now. But there's no phone in the place. However, we're making arrangements for him to return without delay.'

At the Stockholm Police District headquarters, Welander had called together his leading officials.

'Let's have a meeting. And with all this mob scurrying about, there must be someone who can rustle up some coffee.'

Bleary-eyed and dishevelled, Stockholm's top cops gathered around a table. In the background, phones rang incessantly as patrols reported, new instructions were sent out and journalists and news agencies harried the beleaguered police for information on any recent developments.

'From the sound of that bedlam, Holmér must be the only person in the whole country not to know what has happened,' observed Linder drily.

'Can we get down to business?' retorted Welander.

Linder nodded agreement. He produced a piece of paper and read a short report.

'At 20.40 on 28 February, Olof Palme and his wife left their flat at No.31 Västerlånggatan. Palme dismissed his bodyguards, telling them he did not require them any more that day. Then he called his son, Mårten, and they decided to meet at the Grand Cinema. Olof and Lisbeth Palme walked along the street to the nearest subway station, Gamla Stans Tunnelbanestation, where they took a train to Rådmansgatan, three stops along the line. From there, they walked along Sveavägen to the cinema, where Olof Palme bought four tickets after he and his wife had been joined by his son and his girlfriend. The performance ended at

23.00 and, after saying goodnight to Mårten shortly after leaving the cinema, Olof and Lisbeth Palme started to walk down Sveavägen towards Hötorget. At the junction with Tunnelgatan, an unknown man jumped out and fired a pistol. We have established that the Prime Minister was hit at 23.21. As to what followed next, I would ask Detective Inspector Kocí to give a short statement on the actual incident.'

Kocí repeated how the shooting had been reported to him, and the steps which Söderström had taken.

'I take it that none of the patrol cars sent to seal off the exits from Tunnelgatan came up with anything?'

'Nothing,' Kocí answered.

'Linder, what has the Violent Crimes Department found? Anything worth following up?' asked Welander.

'So far, nothing from the scene of the crime, and Chief Detective Inspector Lange has decided that there's no sense in trying to examine the place at night, but in the morning he'll initiate a thorough search of the area. Lisbeth Palme refused to be interrogated by my men at the hospital, and the examination of Palme's body and his clothes has so far given us no fresh leads.'

Sandström spoke. 'You might be able to get something from SÄPO. I heard that Karlsson had got one of their Technical Department teams on the job. They were going to give the Palme home a thorough search for any sort of bugging device. Karlsson's been involved in quite a bit of counter-espionage work, you remember.'

'I suppose it was a prudent move.'

'Well, it seems that Palme's security guards were not told that Palme intended to go to that cinema. Maybe, when he called his son, someone else was listening.'

Welander reached for the phone and got through to Hjälmroth. 'What about the people from your Technical Department?'

'No bugs inside Palme's flat,' answered the head of SÄPO, 'and we also checked the junction box in the basement in case the phone had been tapped from there, but the thing was covered by such a thick layer of dust that my men are convinced it could not have been touched for months or years.'

'Wait a minute,' interposed Welander. 'Olof Palme called his son, Mårten, and arranged to meet him and his girlfriend this evening to go to the movies.'

'Yesterday evening,' corrected Hjälmroth.

'Yesterday evening then. Suppose it was Mårten's phone which had been bugged. That would explain the murderer's knowing where he could attack Palme.'

'We had thought of that,' Hjälmroth answered patiently. 'I've had another squad checking Mårten's flat as well. It's clean.'

'Maybe some intelligence services use new and more sophisticated bugs which you can't detect,' suggested Welander.

'You can rely on us to look into that possibility,' Hjälmroth said coldly. 'May I ask what sort of progress the Stockholm Police District has made towards catching the assassin?'

'We are putting our plans into operation.'

'Very impressive. So, tell me, where have you set up your road-blocks?' asked the head of SÄPO.

'We haven't,' answered Welander.

'What?' Hjälmroth could not believe his ears.

'How could we?' argued Welander. 'We've taken statements from and examined all the witnesses, and, in my opinion, their evidence is absolutely worthless. With no idea what the man looks like, what could the policemen on the road blocks do? Stop every car and every pedestrian? Then what? Ask everyone "excuse me, sir, but did you happen to shoot Olof Palme?" '

'But the airports, the ferries?'

'The same thing applies. It would have been impossible to stop every man who wanted to leave the country because one of them might be a murderer whom we would not be able to recognize even if we were staring him in the face. Be reasonable.'

The man from SÄPO listened in stunned silence.

'So what have you actually done? Anything?'

'Of course. We've sent out information to all the police stations in the country. Then at dawn officers are going to call at every single house in the area, asking if anyone had seen anything which might have a bearing on the murder.'

'How did you send your message out?'

'By urgent, "flash" telex. Don't worry. Everyone will be on the job.'

Hjälmroth sniffed contemptuously. 'And the borders? Are you really going to leave them open?'

Welander hesitated. 'Well, we've given an order that strict controls are to be enforced, and that's being announced over the media. But since, as I say, we have no definite idea what the man we are chasing looks like, we don't really expect anything to be achieved. But what we hope is that, by making a big fuss about the strictness of the checks, we shall get the killer too scared to make a break and he'll stay bottled up in Sweden until we get a lead to work on.'

'That is, if he's not already left without waiting to watch the TV news,' commented Hjälmroth acidly.

'There's already a team of officers detailed to stand by to evaluate all reports from the public and to pass on those which might be of significance,' continued Welander, ignoring the gibe of the SÄPO man, 'and special telephone numbers are being allocated which the public can call with information. Five of our men have been given the task of standing by those phones, and a senior officer will screen the reports. A really thorough search of the scene of the shooting and the whole area round about will commence as soon as the sun is up. Maybe, in the morning, we shall have rather more to go on,' he concluded hopefully.

Welander hung up, and shortly afterwards the meeting broke up. The orders had been passed down. Now, all they could do was to sit back and await developments.

While the Security Police were busy guarding important persons against any possible attacks and checking on suspected subversive elements, and the Stockholm Police District was alerting all the other branches of the national police and setting in train its own measures, such as they were, the news of the death of the premier was seeping out. However, when Swedish television closed down for the night, three minutes before midnight, no-one in the studio had heard anything, so the transmission ended without any announcement. Two of the national radio channels had also gone off the air, leaving only the late-night pop-music programme, presided over by disc jockey Staffan Schmidt.

Between records, Schmidt kept up a quick-fire patter of breezy chitchat and wisecracks, punctuated only by occasional phone calls from listeners. About an hour after Olof Palme had been shot, one of the journalists who had heard the first report by Söderström to the Stockholm Police District Radio Centre called Radio House and broke the news to the switchboard operator.

'Tell Schmidt to interrupt his programme,' urged the reporter. 'I can't understand why you people hadn't got a newsflash already.'

'Sure, sure,' replied the operator. 'Thanks for your call.' Another bloody drunk, she said to herself and ignored the message.

In fact, Radio Sweden had received a newsflash by urgent telex from one of the news agencies, timed at 00.20. It was lying unread in the telex machine in the deserted news studio. The news of Palme's death had meanwhile been transmitted by the BBC and by several American stations, but in Stockholm Schmidt went on churning out pop numbers and was still his usual cheerful self. One of the American stations phoned through, and this time the switchboard did pass the call to Schmidt.

'And here is a listener with a request who is calling all the way from the United States,' crooned Schmidt. 'And a very good evening to you back there.'

'We're trying to tell you that your prime minister has been murdered,' cried the exasperated American announcer.

Those damned crackpots, they have nothing better to do than make stupid transatlantic calls, Schmidt complained to himself. What sort of a kick do they get out of that kind of sick joke? Lucky I hadn't put the call on the air.

The studio clock showed 00.40. As the record stopped spinning, he was ready with another funny story for his listeners.

A few minutes later another Swedish journalist managed to get through to Schmidt with what was now the stale news. The disc jockey was worried. No one was in Radio House who could advise him, and if there was any truth in the report of Palme's death, shouldn't he be playing rather more suitable music? Taking his courage in his hands, he phoned Ove Joansson, Director in Chief of Radio Sweden.

'What ought I to do?' asked the distraught disc jockey.

'Have you any official confirmation?' demanded Joansson.

'No, sir. You see, I'm here on my own,' Schmidt started apologetically.

'You will not broadcast any sensational rumour,' interrupted Joansson gruffly. 'Nothing goes out which has not been officially confirmed. And that's an order. Good night.'

The Director in Chief slammed down the phone and went back to sleep. Schmidt took a deep breath and told a few more funny stories. But now call followed call. It seemed that every journalist in the country knew. Schmidt had to face up to the situation. It was impossible that all these callers were either insane or practical jokers and that they had all conspired to tell the same story. Something had to be done. Schmidt walked over to a safe that stood in the studio and contained material for all possible eventualities. He found a box in which were several tapes on which were recorded six hours of solemn music, entitled 'The King is Dead'. The disc jockey removed the latest hit from the turntable and, without a word of explanation or making any announcement, started to play the first track of 'The King is Dead'.

Staffan Schmidt was not the only person to be alerted by insomniac journalists. One of them had spoken to Jan Ström, a news reporter with Radio Sweden, and he decided to go on duty. In the news studio, he discovered the news agency telex. Within ten minutes he had prepared a statement, and at 1.10 he went on the air.

'This is Radio Sweden, Channel 3. Here is a special news broadcast ... Olof Palme, Prime Minister of Sweden, was shot tonight in central Stockholm and died later at Sabbatsbergs Hospital. This news has been confirmed by the Minister of Finance and the Vice-Premier, Ingvar Carlsson. A meeting of the Government is now in progress. The police are looking for a man of about thirty-five to forty years of age, with dark hair and wearing a dark overcoat. His description has been circulated to all taxi-drivers.' The statement went on to give what was known of the incident and a few facts about the dead premier's career. He had been a few months short of his fifty-ninth birthday.

The transmission then continued with further excerpts from 'The King is Dead'.

Jan Ström's assertion that a meeting of the Government was in session was correct, but there was very little the ministers could do. As soon as Dahlsten got the news of the assassination from Kocí, he had set about assembling a quorum of ministers at the Chancery building. But the absence of the Speaker of Parliament, Ingemund Bengtsson, in his phoneless apartment in Málaga, presented them with a constitutional problem. Ever since the reform of the constitution in 1975, the last vestiges of even apparent authority had been stripped from the King, and it was the Speaker of Parliament who formally appointed the prime minister, who in turn appointed his ministers. Once a prime minister was removed, whether by resignation or death, the authority of his ministers expired and they were obliged to resign. But their resignations had to be handed to the Speaker of Parliament, who would then appoint a new prime minister. In the absence of the Speaker, the best the ministers could do was to prepare letters of resignation and wait for Bengtsson to materialize and for the newly appointed prime minister to select his colleagues in the Government.

Hans Holmér felt refreshed after a good night's sleep. The crisp, clean snow sparkled in the bright morning sunshine. As he took a leisurely shower, the chief of the Stockholm Police District congratulated himself on getting away from the petty problems and aggravations of his office for a couple of days. He had checked in the night before at an unpretentious hotel in the small town of Borlänge. Since no one knew where he was, he could look forward to being left in peace. The sharp mountain air gave him an appetite, and he walked briskly to the breakfast room. As he was striding through the lobby, the clerk in reception was reading a newspaper. He looked up at Holmér.

'Dreadful business, this, isn't it?'

'What?' asked Holmér, expecting to hear some item of local scandal.

'About Olof Palme,' replied the receptionist. 'Haven't you heard?'

Holmér shook his head. 'What about Palme?'

'He's dead, sir. Murdered last night. It's all over the paper. Here, see for yourself.'

He handed the paper to Holmér, who gazed horrified at the shrieking headlines. He rushed to a phone. A few minutes later, the seductive breakfast forgotten, Holmér was in his car, racing back to Stockholm.

The news of Palme's death shocked Holmér deeply. Not only did he respect, even revere, the murdered premier: Palme was also a close friend. As he drove towards Stockholm, Hans Gillis Åke Holmér was consumed by anger and indignation. But he felt that it was fitting that he would be the man destined to track down the killer: for him, the meting out of justice would be a revenge, an act of retribution for the man who had done so much to make his professional life the outstanding success which it undoubtedly had been. And it would be a chance to show Sweden and the whole world that he was indeed worthy of Palme's trust. It was bitterly ironic that the death of his friend and protector should provide him with the opportunity to crown his career with a resounding triumph.

Holmér was fifty-six, a man of the same generation as Olof Palme. When he left school, he had joined the army and become a captain in the Royal Svea Life Guards. But at thirty-two he had resigned, to study law, and after graduating he had become a clerk in the offices of various provincial public prosecutors. Within three years, he had risen to be deputy public prosecutor in Stockholm. The following year, the Swedish police organization was completely restructured: for the first time a directorate of the National Police was formed, and Holmér was appointed chief of one of its divisions.

While the young, ambitious lawyer was rapidly climbing the ladder of promotion in the police, another young lawyer was making a name for himself in his championing of radical movements, notably the offering of asylum in Sweden to American boys who objected to being enlisted to serve in the war in Vietnam. This was the campaign above all others which brought Olof Palme to the front rank of the Social Democratic party. Holmér was also a member of the party, but his reputation was more that of an efficient administrator and technocrat, as opposed to the flamboyant Palme, and their characters neatly complemented each other. As Palme's bandwagon rolled, Holmér clutched tightly onto his coat-tails.

And now Palme was dead. As Holmér drove into the suburbs of Stockholm, he remembered the way he had been given the job of head of the Security Police, back in 1970. The hand of Palme was clearly behind his selection. His experience with SÄPO would stand him in good stead now, he reflected grimly. So what, if it had been a politically inspired appointment? He had done a damned good job, he assured himself. When he took over, SÄPO had been a shambles, a laughing-stock among security forces. It had concentrated on keeping tabs on known Communists and anti-war agitators, but actual spies roamed about virtually unheeded, and news of its failures was stifled under a blanket of secrecy. Holmér had changed all that. He had invited the press to inspect the force and had given interviews freely to journalists. A new image was projected of a band of hard-working and dedicated men with nothing to hide from the Swedish people.

But then there was Persson. Holmér pursed his lips. Karl Persson was the man who, as Secretary of State at the Ministry of the Interior, had created the new National Police Directorate, and then he had become its first Director General, Holmér's boss, for the Security Police in Sweden is, at least nominally, no more than a branch of the national force. Holmér had never got on well with Persson. There had been that scandal over the Minister of Justice, Holmér recollected. No need for all that dirty washing to come out now, he told himself. It would not cast much credit on the memory of his dead friend. It had done for Persson, however; He was now in retirement, an old man still acting as a security consultant to some big companies but with no influence in the police hierarchy. Holmér had come through the episode pretty well. He was uninvolved; he had refused to have anything to do with the dirty tricks aspect, and he had taken up his promotion as head of the Stockholm Police District without attracting any criticism over the affair.

He listened to a news bulletin on the car radio. There was nothing fresh of any importance; the killer was still at large. Holmér collected his thoughts. In a matter of minutes he would be in his office, and from that moment he would be in charge of the manhunt. He must formulate a plan. It struck him that he had practically unlimited resources at his disposal. Every policeman in the country would be eager to catch the assassin, and such was the sense of national outrage that every citizen, whether a supporter or opponent of the late Olof Palme, would be ready to co-operate in tracking down the perpetrator of so atrocious a crime. Whatever he might demand in the way of men or equipment would be granted without question. With a thrill of pride, Hans Holmér was conscious that, for the time being, he had become the most powerful man in all Sweden.

At about the same time, the other missing man, Ingemund Bengtsson, was also on his way home. During the night one of his neighbours had heard the announcement of the death of Palme on the BBC, and he considered that it might be of interest to Bengtsson. The Speaker of the Swedish Parliament found a phone and placed a call to Stockholm. He was informed that the

Foreign Office had already taken action, requesting the Spanish authorities to find him and assist in getting him back to Sweden as quickly as possible. In the early hours of Saturday morning, he was escorted by members of the Spanish security forces to the airport, where Felipe Gonzalez, the Prime Minister, had placed his own plane at his disposal. By eleven, Bengtsson was in the Chancery building, where he formally accepted the resignations which the ministers had prepared the previous night. He requested them to remain at their posts until such time as he appointed the successor to Olof Palme.

The police did not wait for the arrival of their chief before renewing their activity, but neither did the citizens of Stockholm. After the broadcast of Ström's announcement, the news spread like wildfire, and an official press conference was held at five in the morning.

People started to converge on the intersection of Sveavägen and Tunnelgatan. When Söderström had departed with his eight witnesses, he had left the roped-off area guarded by a couple of young and inexperienced policemen. They watched the growing crowd of onlookers with dismay. Most of the people were quiet and orderly, drawn to the spot either by morbid curiosity or by a sense of respect for the murdered man. Inevitably, there were a few nuisances. There were some disturbances, and twice young punks amused themselves by cutting the ropes.

The police were able to control the trouble-makers, but soon they faced a new challenge. A couple of people approached, carrying red roses, the symbol of Palme's Social Democratic party. Sadly and solemnly, they dropped the flowers on the spot where their leader had been shot down. It was a restrained and moving tribute to the memory of a man who was idolized by many of his followers, and the idea of mounting a great demonstration of affection and mourning soon spread. More and more bunches of red roses arrived and were thrown onto the ground, their crimson petals covering the spot where Olof Palme's red blood had stained the snow. The policemen were not happy that the scene of the crime was being inundated by this floral tribute before the specialists had a chance to carry out a full investigation, but how could they interfere with so touching a spontaneous gesture? They stood there, awkward and self-conscious, and prayed that the population of the capital would behave themselves. At half past six, one man came up to them and handed over a bullet which he had found.

Soon, Chief Inspector Vincent Lange arrived with his men from the Technical Department. When his team had first visited the spot at ten past one in the morning, they had looked around for about an hour before abandoning their search until daylight. The policeman handed the bullet to Lange.

'Where was it found?' he asked.

'Over on the other side of Sveavägen, outside the part of the street we have roped off,' answered the policeman. 'Will you be starting your examination of the area now, sir?' he asked.

Lange gazed in despair. Any clues which might have remained were now buried deep beneath a mountain of red roses.

'I'd need a bulldozer to shift that lot,' he commented bitterly, and turning to look at the crowd of several thousands who were now choking the road, he knew that his task was hopeless.

Still, something had to be done, and Lange ordered the cordoning-off of a wider area and demanded that more men be sent to carry out a stringent search, although he was convinced that by now any evidence would have been destroyed. At half past eight an army of disgruntled policemen started to look vainly for more bullets, spent cartridges or traces of where stray shots might have hit buildings. More men arrived, with metal-detectors, to add to the congestion and confusion. Eventually, Lange ordered that all the snow around the spot where Palme was shot should be collected and removed for examination. By now the TV cameras were on the scene, and viewers were able to see twenty-five large plastic sacks of snow and rubbish solemnly carried off. The towering monument of red roses remained untouched. Indeed, as the police continued with their pointless labour, there was a growing sense of resentment in the crowd against them, as if they were in some mysterious way responsible, if not for the tragedy, at least for the farcical aftermath. As a final gesture, a huge street-cleaning machine was brought in to sweep the whole street, from the cinema to where Palme was killed. That yielded another cubic metre of rubbish, but Lange knew that he dared not touch the roses, beneath which was the only patch of ground which might conceivably have been worth examination. It was quarter to four in the afternoon when the teams from the Technical Department quit.

By then, Hans Holmér had assumed command over a force of

300 policemen, all charged exclusively with the task of seeking and capturing the killer of Olof Palme. He had supplemented his own men with no fewer than a hundred of SÄPO's specialist agents, who had to be diverted from other duties. There had been a meeting of the various police chiefs who had all been taking action more or less independently of each other. And he had also held his first press conference. Things were beginning to move – or were they?

3

Megasleuth!

It was in August 1985 that Sven Beckman met Ruth Freeman. He was a serious-minded young journalist, keen to make a name for himself. Perhaps one day he would be the man to uncover a Swedish Watergate; that was his secret dream. Meanwhile, to pass the time until he was presented with Fame and Fortune, he was employed as a junior reporter with *Svenska Dagbladet*, one of the biggest-selling morning newspapers in Scandinavia.

Sven spoke competent but rather formal English, with a heavy accent. While waiting for his Watergate, he rather fancied getting promoted to become Dagbladet's London correspondent, and that was one of his reasons for enrolling as a student at a summer school at Cambridge. It was a vacation course which would give him a whirlwind brush with all aspects of British culture and, better still, would introduce him to many interesting people who would be invaluable contacts when he came to land that London assignment.

That was not the impersonal light in which he viewed Ruth Freeman. A pretty girl with fluffy auburn hair and brown eyes which seemed to be expressing some inner amusement, eyes which virtually chuckled, she appeared to Sven to embody the better features of the British people in a particularly appealing form. Sven had been invited to look up Ruth's parents in London by her aunt, the younger sister of Ruth's mother, who had married Lars Olsson and was now living in Stockholm. At the time of the marriage, Lars had been a manager of the Stockholms Enskilda Bank and had been on a tour of duty with the affiliated Scandinavian Bank in London. With the merger of the Stockholms Enskilda and Skandinaviska Banken, Lars had returned to Stockholm to a senior position in the bank, bringing with him his bride, as a trophy of his campaign in Britain.

Ruth had recently graduated from the University of East Anglia, one of the newer and livelier seats of learning, where she had studied Creative Writing. Now she was looking for a subject on which to write creatively. Instead, she had discovered Sven Beckman. Although he was tall and well built and sported a light fringe of ginger beard, there was something boyish about him which attracted Ruth. It was not that he brought out her maternal instincts: rather he made her feel flatteringly mature, as if her twenty-one years on this planet had brought her wisdom which far outstripped her experience.

When he had completed his short course at Cambridge, Sven had spent a few days with the Freemans, and the two had become friends. After he had returned to Sweden, they corresponded, and when the Olssons invited Ruth to join them for a skiing holiday, she had accepted and planned first to visit Sven in Stockholm. So, muffled up in her thick woollies, clutching a canvas grip and ski-encumbered, Ruth had arrived at Arlanda airport on an early morning flight from London on the Saturday morning after the killing. She was disappointed but not really surprised that Sven was not rushing across the crowded concourse to greet her. The death of Palme had been front-page news all over the world, and, after all, Sven was in the news business.

'If for any reason I miss you at Arlanda, take a taxi to the Sheraton,' he had told her when he phoned a couple of days previously. 'You'll find me in the bar with a drink already poured for you.'

So Ruth pushed her way to the line of taxis outside the airport. A policeman in black-and-white uniform was busy talking to the driver of the first cab, so she went to board the next one, but the policeman motioned to her to wait. Then, with a friendly nod of his head, he walked to the next cab on the line, and the driver of the first taxi packed her luggage into the trunk while she settled back in the black Mercedes. When she told him to take her to the Sheraton, he replied in good English, so Ruth asked about the policeman.

'I suppose it had something to do with the murder of your Prime Minister,' she said.

The driver snorted assent. 'Damned stupid questions! Had I any suspicious fares last night? Well, I ask you, what did he expect? A man holding a smoking gun and demanding to be taken to the airport? What sort of a man are you looking for, I asked him. About the only thing he was sure of was that the guy was wearing a dark overcoat. In Stockholm, in the middle of winter at midnight, everyone is going to be wearing a dark overcoat or a fur, aren't they? I mean to say, if the man had been dressed in nylon stockings and a black bra and panties or a frogman's suit, I might have noticed, but a dark overcoat! If that's the best they can do, they'll never catch the killer.'

Ruth grinned, but the driver relapsed into an indignant silence. As they drove past the Central Station, she looked at the throng of policemen, who paid no attention to arriving passengers but attempted to scrutinize those entering the station. Clambering out of the cab in the windswept Vasagatan, for the first time she sensed, almost like a physical blow, the universal shock and suspense which had gripped the country.

She hurried into the lobby of the Hotel Sheraton. There was no sign of Sven there, nor in the bar. With the help of a receptionist, she phoned his office and miraculously got through to him almost at once.

'I left a message for you at the reception desk. Didn't they give it to you?' he demanded.

'No. What do you want me to do?'

'Come and meet me for lunch at the Marginalen,' he told her. 'It's a restaurant in the same street as my office. Since it's your first day in Stockholm, you had better take a cab rather than venture on the subway. The name of the street is Gjörwellsgatan, but the driver will know the Marginalen.'

'At one?' she suggested.

'Better make it half past, and if I'm not there, take a table and wait for me. I shan't be long, but I have to be at a very important press conference at midday.'

As she hung up, another receptionist smiled at her and enquired whether she happened to be a Miss Freeman, since he had a message for her. She replied that her name was Margaret Thatcher, but would he mind getting her another number in Stockholm? She phoned the Olssons, and ten minutes later her uncle drove up and stowed her and her baggage into the warmth of his Volvo and whisked her to her aunt's house, where she dumped her baggage.

Sven's press conference had been summoned by Hans Holmér in the large assembly hall of the National Police

Headquarters. Holmér had decided to hold it before he had even got back to Stockholm. At ten minutes to eleven, he had hurried into the headquarters building and immediately summoned the officers who had been handling the case pending his arrival. It was striking eleven when everyone had arrived, and Holmér wasted no time with formalities.

'So what the hell has been going on?' he snarled.

Welander told him what they had done and what little progress they had made. Holmér's jaw tightened. These slow-moving, stolid cops needed someone to bite their arses and, by God, he was the man to do it.

'Right,' snapped Holmér, 'the first thing is to get the co-operation of the whole of the people. So, get the press here for a full meeting.'

'When do you want this press conference?' asked one of the junior officers.

'In just one hour's time, so get on with it,' he answered.

'How about the search of the site?'

'Lange is there now,' said Linder.

'Tell him to extend his investigation to cover all the likely escape routes. What about the borders?'

'All exit points are being watched,' Welander commenced, but Holmér interrupted impatiently.

'Of course they are. But have you informed the media, so that the killer knows?'

'I'd already thought of that,' replied Welander. 'The announcement has gone out over all the radio and television stations, and it will be carried by *Expressen* in this evening's edition.'

Holmér nodded. The evening paper *Expressen* had the largest circulation of any newspaper in the whole of Scandinavia.

'Now, what about those witnesses?'

He was told how confused and even contradictory were the statements.

'Interrogate them again. Maybe they'll remember something they forgot to mention the first time. And Lisbeth?'

There was an embarrassed pause. Then Welander said apologetically,

'I'm afraid Mrs Palme is not proving very co-operative.'

'Leave Lisbeth to me,' said Holmér with a wave of his hand. 'Don't forget that I was a close friend of Olof. I know Lisbeth very well. I'll talk to her. Now, gentlemen, I shall tell you what we are going to do.' He gazed round as if to ensure that everyone was giving him their full attention. 'At this press conference, I am going to ask that everyone who was at the Grand Cinema last night call us on special lines. I don't care whether they saw anything or not, they should call. I shall make it clear that we want to talk to everyone, but everyone, who was at the last showing of the movie or was anywhere around at the time. What is more, we want to hear from anyone who saw Olof and Lisbeth at any time during that evening. I want ten officers manning these phones night and day. Then we shall tell the press that we are working on the widest possible front and that we are confident we are soon going to arrest one or more people.'

'Won't that sound unconvincing,' objected Linder. 'The journalists must realize that, if we had the slightest idea of who might be responsible, we would already have detained the suspect?'

Holmér shrugged off so trifling a consideration. 'The man could have gone into hiding. We'll let them understand that we have solid evidence and a definite suspect on whom we're closing in. Once we get the killer nervous, he's sure to make the mistakes for which we shall be watching out. And he certainly ought to be nervous by now,' Holmér added with a grim smile.

If the chief of the Stockholm Police District was expecting an enthusiastic reception of his plan by his subordinates, he was disappointed. There was a definite atmosphere of unease. The men shifted in their seats: in place of assent or applause, there were shy coughs, grunts and sighs. Holmér changed the line of his attack.

'You realize that the Government will be taking a keen interest in the precise steps taken by each and every one of you,' he said pointedly. 'I want every policeman who was on duty last night and who was in the slightest way involved in the investigation to make a detailed written report of his actions. These reports are to be handed to me in person.'

Before the meeting broke up, several more decisions were taken. The head of the Traffic Police was to be contacted without delay and ordered to get from each of the officers who were on duty the night before a list of all important offences reported between midnight and six the following morning. They were also to check on any vehicles which appeared to have been abandoned.

'And get hold of the manager of the Grand Cinema,' Holmér ordered. 'Find out exactly which members of his staff were on duty last night. We must talk to them. The cashier can tell us how many tickets were sold for the performance; perhaps she noticed if someone paid special attention to Palme.'

'OK,' said Linder, 'but you know everyone pays attention to celebrities when they appear in public. I'm sure there were a couple of hundred people who gaped at Palme going into a cinema last night.'

'No matter,' retorted Holmér. 'Nothing at all is to be ignored. From now on I don't want any limp pricks lying about here. I want action! Now, we can go on with this meeting after the press conference. Let's go.'

Sven Beckman was too young to have attended Holmér's sessions with the press when he was opening up SÄPO to public scrutiny. He looked curiously at the stocky figure who strode jauntily into the meeting at the head of the bunch of senior police officers. Holmér's crop of curly fair hair was now almost entirely grey, but his ruddy complexion and energetic gait and gestures gave an impression of lasting youthfulness. A man who knew where he was going and who was absolutely sure of himself, Sven judged.

There were about a hundred reporters and photographers packed into the hall. They listened attentively to the recital of events, but it was when Holmér asked them to emphasize that the police were anxious to interview everyone who had been at the Grand Cinema for the last sitting that they seemed to respond. Here was something definite, and Holmér held their interest when he informed them that one bullet had been recovered from the scene of the crime. This was what they had come for: the stuff of headlines. Then came the questions.

'Do you have a suspect?'

'No comment.'

'Do you suspect any specific terrorist organization?'

'We are working on the widest possible front.'

'Does that mean that you do not have any specific suspect?'

'I did not say that. I don't want to go into details which might prejudice further investigations.'

'Do you think you will ever catch the killer?'

'Definitely. It's only a matter of time.'

'A short time?'

'I hope so.'

'Do you have any idea of the motive for the crime?'

'I can only confirm that we are working on the widest possible front. No possibility is excluded.'

'In your opinion, was the killer a Swede or a foreigner?'

'We do not exclude either alternative.'

'Have you closed the borders?'

'They are not closed, but stringent controls are in operation. Now, please excuse me, gentlemen. I'm sure you appreciate that I'm quite busy at the moment,' smiled Holmér.

And that was it.

The press conference was broadcast live by Radio Sweden. Despite Holmér's apparent confidence, it was obvious to any listener that the police did not have any clue as to the identity of the killer, just as it was obvious to Sven Beckman as he made his way to meet Ruth. The press conference had been managed with such briskness that he arrived at the restaurant quite some time before she appeared. As he sat waiting, he reflected on the answers Holmér had given to the reporters. There was something about the police chief's ebullience which no longer carried conviction, and the young newsman became more and more depressed.

'Well, you don't seem exactly overjoyed to see me.'

Sven jumped up. Standing in front of him was Ruth, a broad grin on her face.

'Forgive me,' Sven was blushing in confusion. 'I did not see you come in.'

'Something on your mind?' she asked.

'Palme.'

She nodded. 'Tell me all about it. I can't understand who would have killed him.'

'Neither can the police, by the sound of what they are saying,' commented Sven. 'But, first of all, of course I am glad you got here. It's great to see you again.' Belatedly, he kissed her welcome. 'Sit down, and let's order. I warn you that the food is not all that hot, but the gravlax is edible. And if you feel like a beer, stick to Pripps Export Class 3. What we call Class 1 and Class 2 beers are a national scandal.'

Ruth looked around her at the plain wooden tables and chairs.

'I like this place: it has atmosphere. Is this where all you busy news-hounds eat?'

'When we get paid,' answered Sven. 'You meet people here at times like this, and there will always be some of us keeping an eye on the comings and goings at that complex of buildings up the street.'

Ruth looked at him questioningly.

'The Soviet Embassy, with its enormous compound,' Sven told her drily.

'Do you think they are behind the murder of Palme then?'

'I don't know. But if they were, I would expect our Security Police would have kept tabs on them. Ever since we caught a Russian submarine which ran aground while nosing around our main naval base, I am sure they must have been kept under special surveillance, although there's a suspiciously large number of so-called diplomats attached to their embassy.'

'I remember the fuss about that. Did Palme make what are politely called "energetic protests"?'

Sven shook his head. 'He was not in power then. He lost the election in 1976. We had a coalition Government of Liberals, Conservatives and the Centre Party – they used to be called the Farmers' Union, and their leader, Thorbjörn Fälldin, was prime minister. There was a lot of publicity about the number of "illegals" cluttering up the Soviet and other East European embassies. Some wag, rumoured to be a member of SÄPO, suggested that, if all the gentlemen who might have some connection with the gathering of intelligence were to be expelled, the only man left in the Soviet Embassy would be Boris Pankin. He's the ambassador,' he added by way of explanation.

'But tell me more about Palme. Was he the sort of man to have a lot of enemies?' Ruth asked.

Sven considered his reply carefully. 'Olof Palme was a controversial figure, especially in as staid and conventional a country as Sweden. You know that Sweden is a neutral country and has been ever since the time of Napoleon, but there is more than one way of being neutral. Palme was very active in supporting Third World countries, independence movements and all that kind of thing.'

'That sounds more likely to annoy the Americans than the Russians,' Ruth commented.

'He annoyed them plenty, especially when he offered asylum

to those Americans who refused to fight in the Vietnam war and again over his sympathy with the Sandanista Government in Nicaragua, but especially when he did a deal with Castro, building ships in Swedish yards for Cuba. The Social Democrats are as conservative in their own way as the Liberals, but Palme appealed to the radical wing of the party, so he ruffled quite a few feathers. Yet I would say that he was a popular Prime Minister.

'You see, he was something very rare in Swedish politics, a man with charisma. And his professed idealism touched a sensitive spot. The Swedish people generally have an uneasy conscience, almost a sense of guilt, at being so prosperous in a world where there is so much poverty. And it is obvious that being neutral during two world wars was highly profitable. Of course, nearly everyone agrees that the only sensible policy for a small country like Sweden is to stay out of the fights of the big powers, but getting rich from their wars has an immoral feeling about it. That was the secret of Palme's success, although I believe he was actually more respected abroad than in his own country. He had something of the radical evangelism of Kennedy, or that was how it looked to a lot of people, and I suppose now the fact that he too was gunned down will convince them of the superficial parallels between the two men.'

'Yes, but you cannot compare Sweden with the United States,' objected Ruth.

'Sweden is a small country, but Palme was a big man,' Sven answered. His expression was sombre.

'When did you hear the news of the murder?' asked Ruth.

Sven laughed. 'About midnight. I was in the office. As we are a morning paper, most of us work during the night. Well, I was keeping up with my English, listening to the BBC, and I heard a newsflash. I called Radio Sweden but they ignored me. You know, I have a feeling that the truth of this affair will eventually be unearthed by some unofficial person, ferreting about, rather than by our legions of bureaucrats and complacent cops.'

'Someone such as a young reporter, for example?' asked Ruth innocently.

'Eat your gravlax,' answered Sven.

Even before Sven Beckman had covered the few metres to the Marginalen, Hans Holmér had reconvened his group of senior police officials and commenced his drive to unmask and capture the criminal.

His first task was to assemble the army of detectives and ordinary constables who would be required in this quasi-military offensive. Every man who could be spared without utterly crippling every other operation was seconded, including the hundred SÄPO men, and a 'Brains Trust' comprising Holmér and six police chiefs was set up to whom all reports were to be submitted. The Ministry of Justice was invited to send two observers. Soon orders began to descend as thick and fast as the snowflakes in the city.

Telephone lines were requisitioned with up to a dozen detectives deputed to stand by the 'hot line' for reports from the public, and an additional four solely concentrating on calls from people who had attended the last showing at the Grand Cinema.

There was no way the Brains Trust could examine all the calls which were anticipated, so a further squad of sixty detectives was given the job of screening them. Every man, woman and child in Sweden was a potential informer: how could the fugitive hope to escape detection? But Holmér was not content to wait passively for the criminal to be brought to him: all suspects were to be traced and their movements checked.

'Where do we start?' asked one of the detectives.

'I'll tell you,' Holmér answered, with the decisiveness of a general about to deploy his troops. 'Palme was a high-profile, public figure, so it is reasonable to suppose that the murderer was a man with a grudge against the Government. Now that sort of person would not have acted suddenly and spontaneously. He would have been nursing his grievance and bellowing about it, probably writing threatening letters to Palme or to the Government as a whole.'

'There are plenty of those. There's a rule by which all such letters are sent to the National Police. We have them in a separate room.'

'Phone down and ask how many letters have been received over, say, the last ten years.'

One of the men called on an internal line.

'Christ!' he exclaimed. 'They get on average 300 a week.'

Holmér was not deterred. Half a dozen men were to start going over them. They, and the twenty-five who were to deal with interrogations, would be assisted by a new computer facility which had to be in place and operational within twenty-four hours.

'Put out a request for a tip-off on anyone who has been voicing a grudge against the Social Democrats or the Government. You know the sort of thing. I am certain our man is out there, letting off steam, and someone is sure to have heard him. Get the announcement made at once. Say that we'll accept anonymous calls, and have five men standing by. Let's see what sort of response we get.'

Linder picked up a phone and gave the order.

Holmér nodded and continued. 'So much for individual crackpots; now let's look into organized opposition. We shall set up a section to collect information on all the political parties and splinter groups who oppose the Social Democrats. There are all sorts of extremists, on both the left and the right, who would be capable of committing acts of violence. There will be plenty of work for this Analysis Group.'

'Shouldn't we also use more conventional methods?' someone suggested anxiously.

'Right, so get a force together to go round all the low dives and lean on known villains. Threaten them, but don't bring them in for petty crimes: we simply do not have the time and resources to cope with the legal complexities. Do a deal with them: we'll turn a blind eye if they come up with some information.'

After consulting the list of men available, forty were detailed for this job. Another ten should start checking the computer records of everyone convicted for a crime of violence and of lunatics who had escaped from an institution. Anyone who had checked into a hotel or hired a car within the past fortnight was to be listed and details entered in a special data-bank for future cross-reference. More men were to go round to Palme's neighbours again to enquire if anyone had noticed anything suspicious.

Linder interrupted this series of staccato commands. 'That's all very well, but, as of now, all we have to go on is one spent bullet and a vague idea of a dark man in an overcoat. Now stop and think. If the killer is a professional, how is he going to behave? He has been seen running off along Tunnelgatan, a man in an overcoat, carrying a gun. Surely the cleverest thing for him to do is to dump the gun and his coat and anything else he might consider to be distinctive, as soon as he is out of sight. Then, provided he has the nerve, he will simply walk back to the junction of Tunnelgatan with Sveavägen. He knows that by now there will be a crowd and he can mingle with it. Everyone will expect him to be running away: the last place they would look for him is among themselves.'

'Yes, but what about those who actually saw him? He doesn't know that no one got a good look at him.'

'No,' replied Linder, 'but he would have heard our cars arriving within seconds, so he would know that by this time the eye-witnesses would have been rounded up and taken back to headquarters for interrogation. One place they will surely *not* be is the scene of the crime.'

'Very well,' Holmér cut in. 'What action are you proposing?'

'Call the City Public Health Department and either get the co-operation of their street-cleaning gangs or else keep them out of the area until our own people have made a thorough search. If we're lucky, round some obscure corner or in a rubbish bin we shall come up with a gun and an overcoat.'

Holmér looked around. 'Anyone object?'

There was silence. That was work for another sixty detectives as well as the city's garbage-collectors.

Holmér took over again. 'I want a couple of officers permanently assigned for liaison with the armed forces and the Government Chancery. And let's take advantage of the latest technology. You know that tiny objects can be spotted from the air or even from out in space. I want the Royal Swedish Air Force to take aerial photographs of the city. And we'll call on the United States for satellite observation of the area. With the high definition of their cameras, a bloodstain or a spent bullet would be easily visible.'

He looked around as if to challenge anyone to contradict him. If Linder or his associates wondered what could be seen by a satellite, hundreds of kilometres out in space, which had not been noticed by police dogs with their noses four or five centimetres off the ground, they were too tactful to say so.

'And we shall make sure the media make a big fuss about how we are using all the most sophisticated techniques,' Holmér added. 'It should keep them happy until we can come up with something concrete. Any other ideas?'

No one spoke: there was a universal feeling that they had quite enough to be getting on with.

'Right,' said Holmér. 'I shall go and see Lisbeth Palme, poor woman. Meanwhile, we get back to our greatest ally, the public. Linder, call and see how many people have phoned in to report suspicious characters since we put out the appeal.'

The police chiefs waited while Linder contacted the switchboard.

'*How* many?' asked Linder incredulously. He turned to Holmér. 'More than 3,000 already.'

'Good God! Put every remaining man on to clearing those calls. Get on with it: we don't have a moment to lose,' barked Holmér, as he strode out of the room.

It takes more than the death of a prime minister to disrupt two successive weekends in any civilized country, and on the first Friday evening in March the roads out of Stockholm were busy with people escaping for a few days from the city. Among them was Sven Beckman. Although Lars Olsson intended to take his family to the more distant ski slopes, he decided that first they should spend a few days at Eskilstuna, a pleasant old town where some of their friends were staying.

'Why don't you ask your young man to join us for the weekend?' he asked Ruth. 'There's plenty of room, and it's not much more than a hundred kilometres from Stockholm.'

'He's not my young man,' replied Ruth.

'Isn't he?' rejoined Lars. 'That's what we used to call it in Britain when I was courting your aunt. Tell me, why are you blushing?'

However, she did phone to invite him. Sven had regretted that his reunion with Ruth had been so fleeting and, as he had several days' leave due to him, he accepted eagerly.

'And I'll tell you the latest on the great Palme investigation when I see you,' he promised.

'Has there been any progress?' Ruth asked.

'A lot has happened, but whether there has been any progress – well, that's not clear,' he answered.

As soon as he could decently get away, he threw a few clothes into a case and bundled it and himself into his slightly ancient SAAB and headed out of town along the road which skirted Lake Mälaren. There was a lot of traffic until he reached the busy little town of Södertälje, where he quit the road to Malmö, forking off to the right, towards Göteborg: he preferred this route, following the shore of the lake, although it was too dark for him to get more than a glimpse of the still water. It was striking seven when he checked into the Sara Hotel. Ruth was waiting in the lobby to greet him, and Sven was gratified that she seemed as pleased to see him as he felt at being close to her again. A few minutes later they were joined by Lars Olsson.

'Let's have a drink at the bar,' he suggested. 'Mary insisted on changing for dinner, so we ought to have time to get a few glasses inside us before she's ready. A couple of friends are meeting us here for dinner,' he explained to Sven. He led Ruth into the bar, a comfortably furnished if rather impersonal room, decorated with modern austerity in a style which reeked of Scandinavian good taste and understatement, while Sven took his bag up to his room. When the young man rejoined them, the conversation inevitably turned to the Palme case.

'I see they caught the creep who did it,' growled Lars. 'It's a pity there's no death penalty in this country: he deserves to be shot.' The morning paper had carried a front-page story of the detention the previous day of a member of a terrorist organization, a man described as a notorious political extremist.

'We can't be sure he did it; he hasn't been tried yet,' protested Ruth. During her time on the campus at East Anglia, she had participated in several student protests against arbitrary arrest in such countries as South Africa, Chile and the Philippines, and she remained convinced that the dawn of an age of tolerance and political liberalism was not too far over the horizon.

Her uncle gazed at her in mild amusement. 'Ruth, dear, this is Sweden, not some savage, jungle state. Our police don't go around beating up kids simply because they have long hair or say things they don't like to hear. You can be certain they wouldn't have taken this guy in if they did not have a watertight case against him. And, remember, there's a special prosecutor already appointed. Now he is a prominent and undoubtedly honest lawyer. If the case against this killer does not hold up, he will order his release. Just think for a moment what a slap in the face that would be for the police and for this man Holmér who's in charge. No, they would never risk making that sort of statement if they were not absolutely positive they had the right man and that they could prove their case in court. Isn't that so, Sven?'

'I very much hope so,' answered the journalist thoughtfully, 'but Holmér is not actually claiming that this is the man who pulled the trigger. They think he's an accomplice, and the hunt goes on for the assassin and the rest of the gang – that is, if there was a gang. You must have seen the photograph in this morning's papers.'

'The police have an actual photograph of the man who killed Palme?' asked Ruth incredulously.

'No,' smiled Sven. 'They have the photograph of a man who did not kill Palme. In fact, it is not even a photograph of a man at all, just an ideal likeness of an unknown person.'

Ruth shook her head in bewilderment. Sven explained.

'Holmér was irritated by the confusions and contradictions in the descriptions given to him by the eye-witnesses. He had heard of a marvellous invention in West Germany, a sort of computer into which you could feed all the information you got from interrogating the witnesses. This machine would then process the data and produce a picture which would be the best possible combination of this input. Well, Holmér is a fanatic for the latest scientific marvels, so he got onto the boys at Wiesbaden and had them fly one of these machines in.'

Olsson picked up a newspaper from a table and peered at the picture. A bland, impassive face stared back at him.

'Why, that could be practically anyone!' he exclaimed.

'That's the trouble,' agreed Sven. 'The police phones have been jammed with calls from people who have identified the photograph as their neighbour, or the butcher, or the school teacher who was rude to little Ingmar. I guess every adult male in Sweden who possesses all his limbs is in danger of being reported to the police.'

'But mightn't publishing this picture of the-man-who-never-was confuse witnesses in future? Ruth said. 'I mean to say, suppose the police have an identity parade, and a witness picks out a man. How can they be sure the witness is not recognizing someone who resembles the photograph rather than the real man they saw?'

Lars Olsson nodded. 'Yes, you're right. Any future identification will be practically worthless. This photograph was a mistake.'

'And there have been some other strange developments,' said Sven.

'Such as?' Ruth queried.

'Well, there was the incident of the second bullet on Sunday. You remember that a man in the crowd found a spent bullet early on Saturday morning and handed it to the police. Since then, Holmér has made a big fuss about his aerial photographs and the satellite which searched the area, but they came up with nothing. Then, on Sunday, there was this mystic, I think he was a guru from somewhere in India, who claimed he could concentrate psychic powers on the problem. He made a show of parading in Sveavägen, and when he squatted down in the middle of the road and then stuck his rump in the air, he attracted a lot of spectators who stopped to watch the fun.'

'What happened? Did he go into a trance?' scoffed Olsson.

'Sure, but don't laugh. He suddenly jumped to his feet, walked quite a distance to one of those refuse bins and pointed. Inside, where no one could possibly have seen it, there was a second spent bullet.'

'Sounds like a lot of nonsense,' grunted Olsson. 'Still, Holmér has a man under arrest; he must be about to close in on the rest of the criminals.'

The arrival of Mary Olsson brought the discussion to an end, and shortly afterwards Lars' friends arrived and the party went in to dinner. Lars Olsson's optimism would have been shaken if he had known that the police had already released the suspect whom they had detained.

But the man was not to be left at liberty for long.

4

The Freak File

As soon as Holmér had sent his staff of senior police officers scurrying off in all directions to cast the dragnet which was to bring in the man or men responsible for the killing, he went to visit Lisbeth Palme. Although she greeted him cordially, he was disappointed that she was unable to give him any clearer description of the murderer. However, he did elicit one useful piece of information. She confirmed that Olof had decided to go to the cinema only ten minutes before they left the flat. She also said that, although her husband liked to slip off informally to a theatre or a cinema, so great was the pressure of work that he had been able to get away only once every eighteen months or so. This effectively ruled out the possibility of a pre-arranged ambush.

Back at police headquarters, the scene was one of mounting chaos. The phones never stopped ringing, mountains of files were being erected and both inside and outside the building thousands of interviews were being held.

Holmér's confident public utterances were based on two convictions: the efficacy of modern technology and the great range of resources, human and material, at his disposal, and secondly his belief that this was a crime which would rapidly solve itself. Some deranged malcontent would boast of his deed or possibly give himself up in the blaze of publicity which he sought. One development which the police foresaw was that not one but a whole flock of mentally unbalanced citizens would fall over themselves in their eagerness to confess to the crime. This always happens after a particularly lurid or sensational murder has hit the headlines: unfortunately, the police have to divert men to investigate each and every such confession, just in case it turns out to be genuine. A typical episode occurred a few days after Palme's murder.

The minister of a church in a suburb of Stockholm called on the special 'hot line'.

'Get over here right away!' he demanded, his voice shrill with excitement. 'I have the murderer of the Prime Minister here, in my office. He has admitted everything to me and is prepared to make a full confession.'

'Does he appear to be violent?'

'Not at all. He is sitting here quite calmly, at peace with himself now that he has wrestled with his soul and resolved to seek forgiveness.'

'OK. Why don't you make him a nice cup of tea? We'll have someone with you in ten minutes.'

So a patrol car was taken off some other task and sent to the church. The miscreant, a man in his sixties, huddled in a shaggy overcoat several sizes too large for him, was driven to Police Headquarters, where he was interviewed by three detective inspectors who might have been more profitably employed. However, the man did not waste any time. Without waiting for them to question him, he burst out, 'It's me. I am the man you have been looking for. I did it.'

'Is that so? Now why do you think we have been looking for you?'

The man wriggled on his chair. 'You are still looking for who killed Olof Palme, aren't you?' One of the policemen nodded. 'Well, that's all right then. I did it. I am the murderer.'

He gazed at them expectantly, but the detectives seemed unimpressed. You might have thought they had men giving themselves up as murderers every day, as indeed they had.

'Well, now, tell us why you did it.'

The man half closed his eyes and gave a faint sigh. 'It came to me in the night. I considered it for a long time before I decided that I ought to obey.'

'Obey whom?'

'Jesus. I had a dream: it was really a revelation. Christ came to me and ordered me to kill Anti-Christ. So I did. Now I am afraid I did wrong.'

'And why do you think that what you did was wrong, if Christ told you to do it?'

'Well, it struck me that perhaps Christ had made a mistake.

After all, he is only human, isn't he?'

'I'm not so sure about that,' replied one of the detectives. 'I don't think he has a national registration number, not in Sweden at any rate. But tell me, how did you actually kill Palme?'

'I did it by telepathy. As one of Christ's apostles, I sent a message to the Archbishop to look after the details. You can ask him. He will confirm everything. So, what are you going to do with me?'

'We have a very special policeman who looks after such top-priority matters. It's too important for ordinary detectives like us.'

The man was handed over to Dr Sundberg, one of the psychiatrists who worked with the police. Just one more harmless crank, but they all took trained detectives away from following up what might have been genuine clues or suspects.

'The fact that a man is a lunatic doesn't mean that he could not have been the killer,' Holmér pointed out when this case and others like it were mentioned at a meeting of the Brains Trust. So a check was made on the movements at the time of the murder of every man and woman certified as insane in the whole country. More men and more resources devoted to a chase which yielded nothing.

'I wouldn't call him a lunatic, but there is certainly one oddball who should be investigated,' remarked Linder. 'Remember the case of the Cobra?'

Holmér nodded. 'Sure, it was only three or four years ago, wasn't it.'

'That's right. On 15 February 1983, to be precise.'

'Who was this Cobra?' asked one of the observers from the Ministry of Justice.

'His name was Bruno Eriksson, but he led us a hell of a chase before we caught up with him,' replied Linder. 'Holger Romander received an anonymous letter, claiming to come from Organization Cobra and instructing him to pick up some documents vital to national security.'

Since Holger Romanader was the Director General of the Swedish National Police, Linder's statement was received with attention.

'So what was in these documents?'

'Romander didn't bother to find out. He simply filed the letter away. There were certain conditions attached to the delivery by Organization Cobra of the documents which the Director General found unacceptable. Anyway, that's a long story; what matters now is to find out where Eriksson was on the night of the 28th.'

That might have been the end of the matter but for the fact that Linder was able to report at the next meeting of the Brains Trust that Eriksson had been tracked down. He was now driving a taxi, and at the time of the killing he had actually been in the vicinity of Tunnelgatan. The observer from the Ministry of Justice was intrigued.

'Well, here you have someone who could have been at the scene of the crime. With a taxi, he had a perfect getaway vehicle. What sort of a man is he? Would he have the nerve to kill the premier?'

'He certainly has the nerve of the devil,' growled Holmér. 'Look, rather than waste time at the meeting, I'll get you his file from SÄPO and you can study it at your leisure.'

'SÄPO? I thought, from the way Linder brought up the subject, that this was something that had been dealt with by the Violent Crimes Division.'

'It's all in the file,' replied Holmér irritably. 'Now, let's get on.'

So, while detectives closed in on Bruno Eriksson, the observer read about one of the most extraordinary attempted *coups* in the recent history of Sweden, or any country.

When Romander did not respond to Organization Cobra's message, a remarkable campaign was launched to compel him to comply. Hundreds of the most important businesses in Sweden received anonymous letters, threatening that their premises would be bombed unless they brought pressure to bear on Romander and forced him to take delivery of the mysterious documents. What impressed the police was the slickness of the operation of intimidation. All these letters were signed 'Organization Cobra', and Linder's Violent Crimes Division, who were in charge of the case, scoured the country to discover a trace of this elusive criminal network, but without success. The affair was considered serious, and in July the fight against Organization Cobra was taken over by SÄPO, which detailed a chief detective inspector, assisted by four detectives, to catch the Cobra.

The threatening letters all ordered the recipients to tune in to certain radio frequencies at stated times, when they would receive further instructions in morse. It was child's play for as sophisticated a force as SÄPO to tune in to these frequencies and to locate the transmitter. Unfortunately, the child was playing a game more complicated than they had realized. What they found when they swooped was merely a relay station which had been receiving a message on one frequency and then retransmitting it on another. However, SÄPO now went along with Organization Cobra, listening to messages and communicating in morse, via the relay station. In this manner, they were able to gain possession of the 'documents of vital importance to national security'.

The nature of the documents was straightforward enough. It was simply a demand for 1,550 million kronor (£155 million). This sum was to be collected by Romander from the hundred leading Swedish companies, their contributions each carefully calculated in accordance with their financial strength. Should Romander or any of the companies refuse to co-operate, a terror campaign would be unleashed throughout the country. To add weight to this menace, the Cobra documents contained descriptions and drawings of various types of bombs which would be employed. Experts confirmed that these details were absolutely accurate technically.

The ingenuity of the men from SÄPO was tested to the utmost, but after a time-consuming watch on pillar-boxes and intense radio surveillance, they succeeded in tracking down Eriksson. They watched him for months, not daring to arrest him for fear that this would prompt the other members of the organization to carry out their threats. Finally, it dawned on them that there *were* no other members: Bruno Eriksson was the entire Organization Cobra.

When Eriksson was detained, the Stockholm Magistrates Court ordered that he should undergo psychiatric tests, and he was confined in a Legal Psychiatric Examination Centre where doctors expressed the opinion that he had attempted this enormous blackmail while under the influence of a psychiatric disorder. The court consequently convicted him of the crime but ordered that he be held in a mental institution until such time as he would be judged to have recovered his sanity. The observer from the Ministry of Justice noted that his recuperation was extremely rapid, and in virtually no time this dangerous, ruthless and highly imaginative man was once more free.

In great excitement, the observer called Holmér to find out the latest developments.

'It's no good,' Holmér told him. 'We've been over his story. He admits he was in the area with his cab, but he had a passenger who has been questioned and who provides Eriksson with a complete alibi for the time of the crime. But I never really thought that it was the Cobra, although he had to be checked. I have my own suspect – you will hear all about him at the right time.'

Had the man from the Ministry of Justice consulted the detectives at SÄPO who had handled Eriksson's case and who had got to know the sort of man he was better than anyone else in the police, he would have been told that they considered him a man incapable of real violence. 'He wouldn't hurt a fly' was their judgement of the 'dangerous' Cobra. They might also have pointed out that he did not bear the slightest resemblance even to the vague physical description of the killer which had been gleaned from the witnesses. But then, as was to become apparent, SÄPO worked on lines very different from Holmér's.

Holmér was now convinced that the killer had not known of Palme's intentions when he left his apartment. Maybe he had been waiting in the shadows, watching the house, and that was one line of enquiry which was being followed by the checking with neighbours and even the staff who had been on duty at the subway station. But it was also possible that it was at the cinema that Palme's vulnerability became exposed. Several hundred members of the audience at the Grand Cinema were painstakingly questioned without any result. Some light was, however, cast by the cashier.

'Yes,' she said, 'I spotted Mr Palme when he joined the queue to buy tickets. I suppose quite a lot of people might have seen him standing in line. He took his turn just like anyone else, and when he got to me, all the seats had been sold. Well, he was the Prime Minister, so I felt it wouldn't be right to turn him away. As luck would have it, there were four places which had been reserved but had not yet been claimed, so I gave them to him. But it meant that he and his wife had to sit apart from the younger couple.'

Holmér pondered this evidence. It would have been possible for Palme to have been observed waiting in line and eventually going into the cinema. The killer would know that he should be emerging in about two hours, plenty of time for him to go home, collect a gun and return to lie in wait for his victim. That line of reasoning led Holmér to suspect that the man he was after was some disaffected Swede, nursing a grievance against Palme or the system, perhaps a disgruntled taxpayer or someone infuriated by bureaucratic bumbling. Of course, there were plenty of people who were discontented with Palme, but surely very few who would be ready to kill him, and even fewer who owned or had access to a gun.

The only other apparent alternative was that this was the work of a professional killer who had stalked his prey. But what would be the motive of such a man? He might be the agent of some foreign power, but there did not appear to be any country with which Sweden was on sufficiently bad terms, and if he had been hired by a terrorist organization, why had no one claimed the credit for the attack? No, while keeping that option open, Holmér was pretty sure that he would find his man among the ranks of home-grown Swedish fanatics. He was confident that, as he had boasted to the press, it was only a matter of time before such a criminal would be caught. The assassin would be proud of what he had done, and what would be the point of such a triumph unless he could tell someone about it? The moment he opened his mouth, he would be betrayed. Every Swede would be eager to inform against him.

There was one more alternative scenario, Holmér conceded. The killer might be a homicidal lunatic. In that case, the probability was that, having killed his victim, he would kill himself: that was a well-established pattern. Perhaps, even now, his body was lying hidden in some garret with a signed confession in his pocket, waiting for someone to stumble upon it. Eventually the stink of corrupting flesh would give it away, but Holmér trusted that it would be discovered long before that.

The detectives who checked on known criminals and informers reported that they had not been able to come up with a single lead, despite every sort of inducement and persuasion. But this failure of his trawling the underworld to bring in anything merely went to confirm Holmér's hypothesis. Stockholm's criminal community knew nothing because the murderer was not one of them.

If the killer maintained a low profile, the same could not be said for his hunter. Holmér wanted to involve the whole of the people of Sweden, and he conducted a public relations campaign which would have done credit to Madison Avenue. While his specialists mounted the spectacular satellite and the 'description machine' operations which were intended to dazzle the men from the media, Holmér called for the files on political extremists from the Analysis Group to be brought to the Brains Trust, for, although the absence of a claim by one of the terrorist or political groups which always sought to publicize their aims by acts of violence should, according to Holmér's logic, have effectively ruled them out, he conceded that he ought to keep an open mind and pursue this line of enquiry in parallel with his hunt for some disaffected individual or homicidal lunatic.

The group, headed by Inspectors Nilsson, Forss and Holm, went hard at it for forty-eight hours, and they could not be accused of lack of thoroughness. Nilsson reported progress to the Brains Trust.

'We are going through foreign political groups, intelligence services and terrorist organizations, as well as private individuals who have made violent outbursts against Palme, but we decided to start with what we consider to be the most promising area, extremist Swedish political organizations,' said the overworked detective, puffy-eyed from lack of sleep.

Holmér waved him away, took the bulky dossier and began to study it. There were disaffected groups from the left who regarded Palme as a traitor who had sold out to capitalism, others from the right who thought him to be a renegade who had betrayed his class and become no more than an agent of international Communism, the friend of Cuba and Vietnam. Other groups were so confused that, beneath their rhetoric, it was anyone's guess whether they were on the left or the right. The inspectors had awarded each group a ranking of low, average or high priority for more intensive investigation.

Most of the extreme leftists, whether they claimed to be anarchists or Marxist-Leninists or tended to Trotskyism, appeared to have regarded Palme as better than any practical alternative and grudgingly to have accepted him. Those who looked to Moscow or to Vietnam for inspiration found no encouragement to launch any act of terror or sedition against the Social Democrats.

The right-wing movements seemed to offer more likely

prospects, and Holmér first considered the rash of neo-Nazi movements with which the country was infected. Typical was RFDU (National Association for Democratic Enlightenment) whose leader, Carl Göran Edquist, had been convicted during the Second World War for 'illegal intelligence', which meant supplying Germany with information about members of the Norwegian resistance. Edquist had participated in neo-Nazi activities: he had published a quantity of pamphlets and carried on a rather skilful series of legal skirmishes against the authorities. He was now too old and crippled to be suspected of being the actual trigger-man, but his followers should be checked. There were probably fewer than fifteen of them altogether.

A similar average rating was given to the Nordic National Party, a giant organization with up to 200 members! This was the more or less official Nazi party, inasmuch as it did nothing to disguise its aims or origins. The group had the habit of sending anonymous threatening letters to prominent individuals, although the threats were never carried out. Its *führer* was Göran Assar Oredsson, a gardener in a small provincial town, but his wife, Vera Oredsson-Lindholm, was a more formidable personality. She was the daughter of the pre-war party *führer* and had attracted notoriety in a court case by her harsh comments about former prisoners of concentration camps. The party had set up what they termed action groups with the aim of causing disturbances and harassment of Jews and others, and they had said that they were prepared to use the methods of the Baader-Meinhof gangs. Democracy does not leave us any other alternative, they proclaimed, taking full advantage of their democratic right of free speech. The inspectors concluded that, like all lunatics, they might be dangerous and should be watched, but they pointed out that, despite its bluster, the party had achieved very little, since each of its scant membership seemed to consider himself a *führer* in his own right – a case of 'all chiefs, no Indians'!

A more nebulous party consisted of Gio Petré, a well-known actress, and Alf Eneström, a doctor, who for ten years had been carrying out a virulent advertising campaign against Palme. It might be worth checking who had sent contributions for that campaign. However, with the death of Palme, the couple were at a loss for a conspicuous target for their abuse. Ironically, they became the victims of their apparent success. This did not prevent Holmér from directing ten to twelve detectives to trail them and keep them under strict surveillance during the following eight months, until the complete lack of any affirmative result finally convinced him that they were utterly irrelevant. Such squandering of police resources was to lead to massive resentment within the force.

The National Party, with perhaps ten or twenty members, headed by a chief detective inspector in a small village tucked away in the south-western corner of the country, merited even less serious attention. It was a breakaway from the National League of Sweden, the oldest and largest of the far-right parties, going back as far as 1915. However, it was only in 1934 that the National League had aligned itself with the Nazi movement, leading to withdrawal of support from the Conservative Party of which it had previously constituted the youth organization. Although three Conservative Party members of Parliament went over to the National League, they lost their seats at the next election, and this was the nearest Nazism ever got to achieving the stamp of parliamentary respectability. None of the groups, not even the National League, could command enough votes to win a single seat.

One after another, the dictators of Germany, Greece, Spain and Portugal, the National League's idols, crumbled into the dust of history, and with the eclipse of Ian Smith in Rhodesia, they were left with only South Africa and Chile as their ideal states. Holmér recalled with wry amusement how Ulf Hamacher, a solicitor, had become the leader of the party, having founded the Swedish-Chilean Society and befriended the Chilean ambassador, who was shunned by all respectable politicians, and had then fled to Chile after he had been declared bankrupt. General Pinochet had granted an audience to his ardent champion but found his proposals on turning Chile into a true Nazi dictatorship unpalatable. Hamacher was refused a residence permit and given thirty days to clear out of the country.

Some of the people who clustered around the National League ought to be checked, but the party was not considered a serious prospect. Low priority was also recommended for the virulently racist 'Keep Sweden Swedish' group, whose main activity had been to infiltrate a couple of members onto the National Board of Immigration.

A higher priority was awarded to *Stoppa Knarket*, a magazine ostensibly devoted to stopping the drugs trade. It was well produced and gave the impression of being a thoughtful publication, until one came to read it. For example, it 'proved' that Olof Palme, a member of the royal family and a woman judge in the Svea Court of Appeal were wholesale dealers in heroin. The proof was a rigmarole of nonsense derived from the conviction of a Lebanese in 1982. The parents of his Swedish wife were alleged to have an undefined connection with a broker who kept his account with a leading Swedish bank which in turn banked with Hambros in London, and, since Hambros had an office in New York, the centre of the heroin trade, the case was proved. If that were not sufficient, the magazine pointed out that the broker had shares in Skandia Insurance, of which Claes Palme, Olof's brother, was a director.

What led Palme to take *Stoppa Knarket* more seriously than its fantastic hotch-potch of unrelated facts and specious absurdities would justify was the disclosure that the bright young men who ran the magazine were members of the Europeiska Arbetar-partiet – the European Workers' Party.

Stoppa Knarket was, in fact, merely one of a number of cover organizations of the EAP. There was also the Anti-Drugs Coalition, which condemned the whole hippie cult, the Academy for Humanist Studies, devoted to conventional culture and classical music and also bitterly anti-hippie, and the splendidly idealistic Livets Klubb (Life's Club), an international body dedicated to the right of all individuals and all nations to survive. Each proved to be merely a cloak for the EAP, as did the Association for Fusion Energy and a group with a programme for developing industry in the Third World, Industry, Freedom and Development. Försvar Nu (Defence Now) exhibited a more militant face of the EAP, proclaiming the necessity for stronger military forces to defend Sweden. As its entire membership consisted of the chairman and the secretary, its influence was rather limited. Yet, behind each of these diverse movements, none of which amounted to anything on its own, stood the shadowy presence of the EAP.

Holmér pushed the file aside. The other movements could wait.

'Bring me everything we have on the EAP,' he ordered.

*

'Is she pretty, this girlfriend of yours?' Ruth asked. Her tone was casual, but there was a hint of sharpness beneath her surface unconcern.

'I tell you, she is not my girlfriend,' retorted Sven. 'It happens that we went to the same school and we kept in touch; you know the way it is.'

'How should I know what sort of relationship you have with her?' Ruth said. 'And you haven't answered whether she is pretty or not.'

It was the evening after Sven's arrival at Eskilstuna, and they were sitting in the hotel lounge before going in to dinner.

'What's this, a lovers' quarrel?' demanded Lars Olsson, who had walked in and overheard the last few words.

Both Ruth and Sven glared at him, but he bestowed a winning smile on them, and Sven shook his head impatiently.

'I was simply telling Ruth that I know a girl who works in Svensson's office, and she has told me a few things about the way the Palme inquiry is going. It's a purely professional interest,' he said to Ruth sternly. Then he added, 'And she has bad teeth and a blotchy skin.'

'Well, perhaps you can tell me what the hell is going on,' Lars said. 'No sooner do they catch this fellow with all that hullaballoo than they release him. What are they playing at?'

'He was only taken in for questioning but I don't think he's in the clear yet,' replied Sven. 'But you know Svensson; he won't want to do anything rash.'

'Who is this Svensson?' asked Ruth.

'He's the public prosecutor who has been charged with preparing the case against whoever is charged eventually with the murder of Palme,' answered her uncle. 'We handle our criminal investigations a bit differently in Sweden from the way you do things in Britain. As soon as the police have a suspect, a public prosecutor is appointed, and from then on the investigation is his responsibility, and the police have to work with him. Because of the importance of the Palme case, and to make sure there would be no unnecessary delay when Holmér had a suspect, a public prosecutor was appointed immediately.'

'Last Saturday, only a few hours after the murder,' Sven confirmed. 'You see, there is always a prosecutor on call, night and day. Whenever the police pull in a suspect, one of the public prosecutors has to be appointed at once. The duty prosecutor that night was a Marianne Lundgren, and as soon as she heard the news, she called the police to see if they wanted her to come in.'

'When would that have been?' asked Mary Olsson, who had quietly joined the group while Sven was talking.

'About three,' Sven replied. 'She spoke to Linder, the head of the Violent Crimes Division, since no one could find Holmér, and he told her there was no need. After all, they had no suspect and there was nothing she could do. At six that morning, she had a routine briefing on the night's events and was again told not to bother to come to Police Headquarters, so she handed over to another prosecutor at nine that morning as usual. This was another woman who was a junior prosecutor, and she decided on her own initiative to call on one of her seniors. That was Svensson, who in turn advised the head of the Public Prosecutor's Office, a man called Claes Zeime, and he at once took charge. Of course, by then Holmér had heard the news and was racing back to Stockholm from his ruined weekend skiing. By the time he arrived, Zeime had spoken with the Attorney General. The Government had met and decided not to wait before appointing a prosecutor. They agreed that Svensson was the most suitable man to take over. He is one of the most senior and experienced of the prosecutors attached to the Stockholm office, but, from what Lena tells me, there could be some tension between him and Holmér.'

Lars Olsson raised his eyebrows. Sven drew his chair closer and lowered his voice. 'What I am telling you must be treated as confidential, although I suppose it will all come out one day. Anyway, when Svensson was appointed, Holmér, as the officer in charge, briefed him on the police inquiry. That was normal procedure. What was not normal was that shortly afterwards one of the bosses of the Security Police, SÄPO, also visited Svensson and quietly gave him quite a different briefing.'

'And your old school buddy eavesdropped?' suggested Ruth.

'Well, she was in and out of the office with papers and coffee, so she did get a very good idea of what was said. Apparently, the boys in SÄPO are unhappy about the way Holmér's setting about the case. They think he's more intent on getting good publicity than actually catching the criminal.'

'Sounds like a squabble between two branches of the police,' said Mary.

'Not really. According to SÄPO, the older and more experienced detectives in Holmér's own Stockholm Police District are also saying that he's not really competent. He's a good administrator, a desk man, and always has been, when he was himself a prosecutor for a year or so and also when he headed SÄPO. What is needed now is a man with practical experience in the field, not someone who's obsessed with gimmicks, such as his satellites and identity machines.'

'I didn't think much of the machine, with its phantom face,' agreed Lars.

'What puzzles me,' put in Ruth, 'is, since no one is said to have seen the man's face, what information did they have to feed into the thing?'

'That is typical of what has been going on, or so I'm told,' replied Sven. 'The morning after the murder, a girl got in touch with the police to say that she had seen a man walking in the street about forty minutes or an hour after Palme was shot.'

'At the scene of the crime?' asked Ruth.

Sven shook his head. 'No, but only a few hundred metres away. She thought he looked suspicious, and he was wearing a dark overcoat. There was nothing actually to connect him with the crime, but the girl remembered what he looked like and, being an art student, offered to draw a likeness for the police. And that was the material from which their phantom face was produced.'

What Lena had not been able to tell Sven was that the man whose computerized portrait had been splashed all over the newspapers was not the man who had been detained. After Holmér had studied the file on the European Workers' Party, he had applied to Svensson for permission to have certain telephones tapped. This necessitated getting approval from a court but, as Svensson had habitually acted for SÄPO in similar cases, he had no difficulty in this delicate matter. Members of the EAP had produced car-stickers with such subtle slogans as 'I would rather eat a plateful of worms than watch Palme on TV' or 'A new Palme is born every day: wear a condom', so it was not surprising that the police were soon listening to phone conversations in which EAP members and sympathizers exulted over the premier's death. That was how Holmér's Brains Trust was able to narrow down their list of suspects and bring in a thirty-three-year-old man for questioning.

It had been done without any ostentation. A couple of ordinary policemen knocked on the door.

'Mr Gunnarsson?' The man blinked and nodded. 'We'd like you to come with us to Police Headquarters. We would be interested to hear your answers to some questions.'

They waited while Gunnarsson put on his coat, then ushered him into the car. The request had been framed as courteously as if the man were being invited to take tea with Holmér instead of facing assertions that he had been involved in the most sensational crime to have been committed in Sweden for 200 years. However, Holmér's triumphant announcement to the press that a man had been detained naturally hit the headlines.

Karl Gerhard Svensson waited impatiently for a report from the police. He was a meticulous man, noted for the sound, methodical preparation of his cases and for his succinct, straightforward presentation of them. He had some qualms about Holmér's boisterous impulsiveness, and he called the Police Headquarters, only to be informed by Holmér that Gunnarsson had already been released.

'But don't you worry,' the police chief assured him. 'We just need a few days to put together all the evidence. Then we'll have him in again.'

'You are sure he is your man then?'

'Absolutely. But there's no point in trying to hold him until we've got our case ready. Otherwise he'd be applying to the courts to be released, and I dare say you would have to let him go as if he were innocent and we'd be left looking stupid. I'll call you in the next few days.'

Holmér was as good as his word. On 12 March, Åke Viktor Gunnarsson was once more in police custody and this time formally told that he was suspected of being guilty of a crime. There was the now familiar fanfare to the press, and a dossier was handed over to Svensson.

The prosecutor read the police submission carefully. The suspect was one of the EAP zealots, and when his flat was searched, it contained a quantity of EAP anti-Palme literature. Gunnarsson, who lived on his own, was not regularly employed, but he worked occasionally as a guard with a private security firm: he was acquainted with the bosses. His hobby was firearms, and he was a member of a shooting club. He possessed a pistol and was proficient in its use. People who knew him considered him a bit odd, wrapped up in his own thoughts and something of a loner without any really close friends. Svensson judged all that to be highly circumstantial, but there were two much more damaging pieces of evidence. When asked where he was on the night of Palme's death, Gunnarsson admitted that he had gone to a cinema. Not the Grand, but one in Kungsgatan, just round the corner. He had gone to the late-night performance and entered after the programme had started at midnight, so he could have been in Sveavägen at the time of the murder. The police had removed some of his clothes from his apartment: examination had revealed powder burns on some of his clothing, consistent with the discharge of a pistol.

The police persuaded Svensson to allow them to hold their man for the full five days which the law permitted before obliging them to get an order from the court to enable them to continue to keep him in custody. When their dossier was handed over to Svensson, he considered it sufficiently convincing for him to write to the court on 17 March, requesting that Gunnarsson be retained for a further fourteen days, during which time the police would be able to press ahead with the accumulation of further evidence. In accordance with normal procedure, the court ordered that he and the prisoner, with his counsel, should appear before them two days later at a hearing, when the public prosecutor would put forward his reasons for requesting Gunnarsson's continued detention. There was absolute consternation when, a few hours before the court was due to convene, Svensson notified them that he was withdrawing his demand and ordering the release of the prisoner. The press besieged Holmér and clamoured for a statement.

Holmér was only too ready to oblige them.

'Letting the man go was a mistake,' snarled the police chief.

'Are you saying you are *sure* that this man was the murderer?'

'He was suspected of being an accomplice,' answered Holmér.

The pressmen were stunned. The earlier statements had not made clear that the man detained was not the actual killer, as they had naturally assumed and as the evidence, of whose nature they were ignorant, had supposedly borne out.

'But are you going on investigating this man then?'

'Yes, I am. I'm ninety-five per cent sure that he is guilty.'

The men from the media would have been happier if Holmér's certainty had stretched to a hundred per cent. As Holmér's daily utterances grew ever more strident, they began to press the reticent Svensson for an explanation, but he remained aloof and silent. The reporters were puzzled, but what was clear was that there was a head-on collision between him and Holmér. One or other of them would have to retract – or quit.

The Government also were aware of the implications, and a conference was called at the Ministry of Justice, presided over by the minister, Sten Wickbom. Holmér, grim-faced, marched into the room accompanied by the two members of the Brains Trust who had been appointed by the Ministry of Justice as observers. One of Wickbom's secretaries joined them at the table as the door opened and Karl Svensson entered. Tall, broad-shouldered and with the fresh complexion of a farmer, he was not a man to be intimidated by the outbursts of Holmér or by the weight of the minister's authority. In contrast to the police chief's neatly cut suit and fashionable shirt (Holmér was something of a ladies' man and dressed accordingly), the prosecutor wore a blue blazer and a knitted tie which might have been the handiwork of his wife, the informal clothes which he even wore in court. Paradoxically, it was the prosecutor, with his free and easy manner of dress, who was renowned for his stubborn orthodoxy and correctness of procedure, while his conventionally clad adversary presented the image of the dynamic man of action who scorned the creaking machinery of the legal bureaucracy whose inefficiency threatened to let a dangerous criminal escape.

Wickbom, a former appeal court judge, attempted to lower the brooding tension between the two men.

'Let us begin, gentlemen. I have asked you here for an informal exchange of views and information. This is a grave matter: we must decide whether the police or the prosecutor have sufficient resources, bearing in mind the difficulties of their tasks. Now, I understand that Mr Holmér wishes to lodge a complaint.'

He cast an enquiring glance at Holmér, who had already leaped to his feet. He spread his arms in a sweeping, theatrical gesture.

'It is not just I who have a complaint; it is the whole of the

Swedish people. We are faced with a crime so dreadful that it has shocked every man and woman in the country, and they cry out for the mystery of who committed it to be solved immediately. It is intolerable that any obstacle should be put in the way of bringing the brutal killer to justice. That is my job, and in order to carry it out I demand complete co-operation, a hundred per cent co-operation – no, 150 per cent!'

'The correct procedures of the law must be observed,' interposed Svensson.

'I am not prepared to waste my time, quibbling with the prosecutor on details like the niceties of some of our interrogations of witnesses, for example. In all such matters, I take full responsibility,' thundered Holmér.

'May I remind you that it is the prosecutor who is the leader of a criminal investigation,' countered Svensson. 'Of course, we want to solve this crime and to do so as speedily as possible, but not at the risk of harming innocent people: that is not justice, and I refuse to be a party to persecution.'

'Persecution!' snorted Holmér. 'The man is as guilty as hell, and you set him free.'

'You had no case ...'

'Of course I had a case!' shouted the enraged police chief. 'The court would have granted me a fortnight to extract vital evidence, but you saved Gunnarsson from facing the interrogations which would have proved decisive. It was obvious to any trained policeman that the man is guilty. Just look at the way he used to skulk about on his own, talking to no one and only going off to that club of his to fire his pistol incessantly at targets, in each one of which he saw the features of Olof Palme.'

'You cannot convict a man for eccentricity.'

Holmér waved Svensson's objection aside. 'And look at the literature we found in his home. The EAP is a filth-factory, and he is immersed in filth.'

'Nor for his opinions, no matter how objectionable,' Svensson continued unperturbed.

'Gentlemen,' intervened the minister, 'let's get back to the facts. What puzzles me is how the prosecutor could be convinced that there was a *prima facie* case against Gunnarsson on the 17th and could already have changed his mind by the 19th. What happened in this period?'

'What happened was that I became aware of certain evidence

which the police had suppressed.' Svensson's voice was icy, but none could doubt the passion beneath the surface. 'If I had been in possession of this evidence on the 17th, I would never have permitted the case to be brought to court.'

Holmér made as if to interrupt, but Wickbom stopped him. 'I think we had better hear what the prosecutor has to say,' he said. 'Please continue.'

'You have been told that Gunnarsson had powder-flash marks on some clothes, yet the killer of Palme was wearing an overcoat; but let that pass. Since we know that Gunnarsson's hobby was pistol target practice, the presence of the marks is not surprising. They were merely corroboration, taking into account the availability of a pistol and his being in the vicinity of the murder somewhere about the time of its being committed. What the police knew and deliberately withheld was, first, that the powder marks on Gunnarsson's clothes were of a type different from those on Palme's after he had been shot, so they could not have had any connection with the crime. Next, it is true that Gunnarsson has access to a gun, but we were not told that it is not the same type as that which killed Palme, and anyway it is kept under lock and key in his club and was not in his possession on the night of 28 February. Once I learned these facts, I immediately ordered Gunnarsson's release. His detention was a miscarriage of justice, and the printing of his name and photograph in a newspaper a serious offence.'

Wickbom frowned and his assistant whispered to him that a paper in the south of the country which supported the Social Democratic party had published these details.

'Never mind the damned paper!' cried Holmér. 'That wouldn't have been too much of a problem if you hadn't let Gunnarsson go free. As for this so-called important evidence, of course I'd taken it into account, and that's why I was proposing to charge Gunnarsson with being an accomplice rather than the man who pulled the trigger.'

'But you still do not know who did pull the trigger,' said Wickbom.

'No, but I probably would have known by now if I had been allowed to continue with the examination of Gunnarsson. Now a crucial line of enquiry has been snapped, through this officious interference. I repeat, I demand from the prosecutor full co-operation.'

'Which you will receive,' Svensson replied smoothly, 'when you present me with a suspect against whom you have managed to find even embryonic evidence. I am utterly convinced that the man you have paraded as your prime suspect is innocent, and I refuse to go further with his prosecution. You seem to be ignorant of the fact that the purpose of the law is as much the protection of the innocent as the pursuit of the guilty and that bringing this man into court and having the case laughed out would damage the cause of Swedish justice and fair play as well as your own investigation.'

'And you seem to forget the exceptional nature of this case which therefore has to be pursued by exceptional means!' Holmér thumped the table violently, but his opponent was not to be cowed.

'Such as practically daily press conferences or television interviews?' he asked.

'I am relying on the co-operation of the whole of the public, and the people are responding magnificently. All except the public prosecutor.'

'I agree with Mr Holmér that this is an exceptional case,' said Svensson calmly. 'So, under the circumstances, wouldn't the logical thing be to hand it over to SÄPO, who are skilled in such matters?'

'But I already have a hundred of SÄPO's best men working under me,' retorted Holmér.

'Exactly. They are working according to your methods, not those of SÄPO.'

'Are you questioning the competence of the National Police?' asked Wickbom.

'Not at all in dealing with normal offences, but it is the head of the Stockholm Police District himself who has pointed to the exceptional nature of this case. Let me ask him a question which I think is relevant to his manner of handling this enquiry. This so-called phantom picture which your splendid machine concocted. We know now that it is based on the drawing you got from a girl who saw a man in a dark overcoat. Where and when?'

'At Birger Jarlsgatan anywhere between forty minutes and an hour after the killing.'

'Just so. But it takes only five minutes to walk from Tunnelgatan to Birger Jarlsgatan, so what was the murderer supposed to have been doing all that time? Waiting to be arrested? No, it is obvious that the girl saw some harmless pedestrian, probably trying to find a taxi at that unearthly hour of the morning, and your splashing the picture all over the country has prejudiced your investigation. So please, let's not hear any more about co-operation, but concentrate on getting some professionalism into this case.'

Wickbom called them to order. 'That's enough, gentlemen. I do not pretend to be qualified to judge on how the investigation should proceed, but I do insist that the two of you come to some understanding on a *modus operandi*.'

'We are obliged to work with whatever clues we can obtain, using every means at our disposal, no matter how unconventional,' Holmer insisted, but Svensson cut him short.

'I am prepared to continue with the prosecution of this case only on the following conditions,' he said, rapping out each word with heavy emphasis. 'First, there must be no more concealing of evidence. Second, the law will be observed absolutely and without any qualification. Third, all future interrogations will be carried out in strict accordance with the rules which have been laid down. This is particularly important if fresh suspects are brought in. I demand an undertaking from the head of the Stockholm Police District that these conditions will be observed and fully respected.'

Everyone looked at Holmér, who shook his head in annoyance. 'Let's get things clear. I have to carry out the investigation, and I shall do it my way. Of course, as soon as we have detained a suspect, the public prosecutor will be informed, as the law demands.'

'That is not good enough. I must be kept fully informed of what is going on, so I insist on daily reports from the police. If I am not provided with full and immediate information, it will be impossible for me to carry out my duties conscientiously: in that case, I shall be obliged to withdraw from the case.'

Svensson looked at Holmér, but the police chief remained silent.

Wickbom shook his head sadly. 'I deeply regret that you two gentlemen are not able to come to the sort of understanding which would ensure this urgent matter being handled harmoniously and without acrimony. I must tell you that the Government has made a formal decision that the police must be given our unquestioned support, and therefore it is up to Mr Holmér to continue his investigation in whatever manner he thinks fit.'

Svensson got to his feet. 'There is no more to be said. I shall give formal notification to the Attorney General of my resignation from this case. Good day, gentlemen.'

With a brief nod to Wickbom, Svensson walked out of the room.

Olof Palme

Hatred. Caricature of
Palme from a right-wing
extremist publication

The mountain of roses heaped on the spot where Palme was killed

The funeral cortège

Iraqi defector, Majed Husain,
murdered January 1985

Iraqi agent, Jamila Mustafa El-Chafej,
cited for her involvement in murder of
Majed Husain

'Phantom No 1.' Computer
onstruction of killer, originally stated
be from eye-witness descriptions,
admitted to be based on impression
an art student who never saw him

'Phantom No 2.' Computer
reconstruction of killer from
descriptions by people who
thought they had seen a man
possibly shadowing Palme

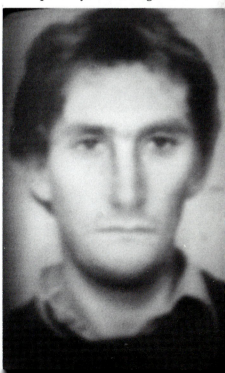

RIKSPOLISSTYRELSEN

Rikspolischef
Holger Romander/GK

Datum
1985-04-02

Diarienr (åber vid korresp)

Utrikesdepartementet
Box 16121
103 23 Stockholm

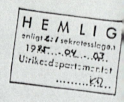

HEMLIG
enligt 2:1 sekretesslagen
1985...04...03..
Utrikesdepartementet
..........KO..

Information ang mordet på irakiske medborgaren Majed Husain 510927-

Husain inreste till Sverige 1983 och ansökte om politisk asyl.
I samband därmed uppgav han att han tidigare varit verksam
vid den irakiska underrättelsetjänsten, men att han lämnat
denna och nu befann sig på flykt undan sin forna arbetsgivare.

Husain bragtes om livet i Stockholm den 9 januari 1985 efter
att några veckor tidigare i tidningen Svenska Dagbladet ha
berättat om sin bakgrund.

Den 17 mars 1985 anträffades kvarlevorna efter Husain. Kroppen
hade styckats och förpackats i två resväskor som gömts i ett
skogsområde i Grödinge, söder om Stockholm.

Företagen utredning har visat att Husain lockats till en lägenhet
i Domus studenthem, Körsbärsvägen 1, Stockholm. Såväl mordet
som den därpå följande styckningen torde ha ägt rum i lägenheten.

De fakta som hittills framkommit i ärendet lämnar inte något
tvivel om att mordet utförts av den irakiska underrättelsetjänsten med stöd av tjänstemän vid irakiska ambassaden i
Stockholm. Misstänkta för brottet är f.n en ung arabisk kvinna
samt två män som inrest på irakiska diplomatpass. Den lägenhet
där brottet har begåtts var vid brottstillfället förhyrd av
den irakiska ambassaden i Stockholm.

Den kompletta förundersökningen rörande mordet på Husain kommer
att tillställas utrikesdepartementet så snart den färdigställts.
Rikspolisstyrelsen vill dock redan nu fästa departementets
uppmärksamhet på det förhållande att den irakiska representationen
i Stockholm kan bindas till det uppmärksammade mordet på Husain.

RIKSPOLISSTYRELSEN

Holger Romander

Holger Romander

./. Persondata betr de personer som misstänkes för mordet
samt PM ang irakiska ambassadens koppling till ärendet.

Postadress
Box 12256
102 26 STOCKHOLM

Telefon
växel 08-769 70 00

Telefon
direktval 08-769.....

Telex
19872 RPS STH S

Memorandum from Romander dated 2 April 1985, stating Iraqi
embassy involvement in murder of Majed Husain

RIKSPOLISSTYRELSEN

Rikspolischef
Holger Romander/GK

Datum
85-12-06

Utrikesdepartementet
Box 16121
103 23 Stockholm

HEMLIG
enligt 2:1 sekretesslage.1
19.85.-12.-07.
Utrikesdepartimentet

EXP till

Pol III

SSB

KABS

POLCH

UTR MIN

Mordet på irakiske medborgaren Majed Husain 510927

Enligt vad Rikspolisstyrelsen erfarit har irakiska
vederbörande förväntat sig en svensk reaktion i anledning av mordet på Husain. Då sådan reaktion ute-
blivit har den svenska passiviteten av irakiska vederbörande tolkats som ett tyst gillande från svensk
sida av de irakiska åtgärderna.

Utifrån de säkerhetssynpunkter som Rikspolisstyrelsen
har att företräda framstår en kraftig svensk reaktion
mot Irak i anledning av mordet på Husain som i hög
grad önskvärd.

Rikspolisstyrelsen har vidare noterat en icke obetyd-
lig ökning av den irakiska underrättelseaktiviteten
i Stockholm under senare tid. Rikspolisstyrelsen
förordar utvisning av Salam Noufan Abid och Salah
Shatab vilka för närvarande leder den irakiska
underrättelseaktiviteten i Stockholm.

RIKSPOLISSTYRELSEN

Holger Romander

./. häktningspromemoria samt tingsrättens
beslut om häktning av en av de inblandade

Postadress
Box 12254
102 26 STOCKHOLM

Telefon
växel 08-769 70 00

Telefon
direktval 08-769

Telex
19872 RPS STH S

Memorandum from Romander dated 6 December 1985,
demanding expulsion of Iraqi 'diplomats'

Rätten	Chefsrådmannen Mikael af Geijerstam
Protokollförare	Barbro Holm
Åklagare	Chefsåklagaren K.G. Svensson, närvarande
Misstänkt	1 Libanesiska medborgaren Jamila Mustafa El-Chafej, ej tillstädes. 3
Offentlig försvarare	Advokaten Klas Kanegärd, närvarande
Tolk	-
Övriga närvarande	Utredningsmännen kriminalkommissarien Inge Reneborg och krimininspektören Per-Olof Palmgren.
Saken	Misstanke om medhjälp till mord

Förhandling

Åklagaren yrkar att El-Chafej måtte häktas såsom på sannolika misstänkt för medhjälp till mord. Skäl föreligger antaga att h̶a̶n̶ ̶k̶a̶n̶ ̶k̶o̶m̶m̶a̶ ̶a̶t̶t̶ ̶ undandrar sig lagföring eller straff.

Försvararen **vill avvakta** med att ange sin inställning till yrk till dess han fått del av åklagarens framställning till grund häktningsyrkandet.

Åklagaren hemställer att förhandlingen hålls inom stängda dörr

Kanegärd förklarar att han ej har erinran däremot.

Tingsrätten förordnar att förhandlingen i fortsättningen hålls inom stängda dörrar, vilket tillkännages.

Utöver åklagaren och Kanegärd är Reneborg och Palmgren närvarande.

Vad som härefter förekommer är redovisat i aktbilaga 19 och 20, som bifogas detta protokoll.

Tingsrätten förordnar att vad som antecknats i aktbilaga 19 och 20 jämlikt 5 kap 4 § rättegångsbalken ej får uppenbaras.

Kanegärd förklarar att han ej ifrågasätter riktigheten av uppgifterna i aktbilaga 19 och 20 samt att han överlämnar häktningsfrågan till rättens bedömande.

Sedan det tillkännagivits att förhandlingen åter är offentlig avkunnas följande

B E S L U T

Jamila Mustafa El-Chafej är på sannolika skäl misstänkt för medhjälp till mord.

Det kan skäligen befaras att hon undandrar sig lagföring eller straff.

På grund härav förklarar tingsrätten Jamila Mustafa El-Chafej häktad i sin utevaro.

Talan mot häktningsbeslutet förs särskilt.

Förhandlingen pågick kl. 15.00-15.25.

Som ovan

Prot. uppsatt s.d.

Court order for the arrest of Jamila Mustafa El-Chafej

RIKSPOLISSTYRELSEN

Rikspolischef
Holger Romander/AC

Datum

86-02-18

Diarienr (åber vid korresp)

HEMLIG
enligt i /sekretesslage
19.86.02.18
Utrikesdepartem.

Utrikesdepartementet
Box 16121
103 23 Stockholm

Mordet på irakiske medborgaren Majed Husain 510927

Med hänvisning till tidigare framställningar i rubr.
ärende önskar Rikspolisstyrelsen lämna vissa komplette-
rande upplysningar:

Rikspolisstyrelsen har erfarit, att irakiska vederbörande till Iraks härvarande ambassad meddelat, att
vid Utrikeshandelsminister Hellströms nyligen timade
besök i Bagdad affären Majed Husain inte togs upp
till diskussion från svensk sida, än mindre framfördes
någon form av protest och att man från irakisk sida
tolkar den uteblivna svenska reaktionen som ett god-
kännande av den irakiska aktiviteten i anseende å
mordet på Husain.

I anledning av vad som sålunda inhämtats vill Rikspolisstyrelsen på det bestämdaste framhålla, att
utifrån de säkerhetssynpunkter Rikspolisstyrelsen har
att företräda, den irakiska tolkningen av den uteblivna
svenska reaktionen icke kan godtagas. Mot nyss angivna
bakgrund framstår en kraftig svensk reaktion mot
Irak i anledning av mordet på Majed Husain som ytterst
angelägen.

RIKSPOLISSTYRELSEN

Holger Romander

EXP t

UTR MIN
KABS
POLCH
POL III
SSB

Postadress
Box 17256
102 26 STOCKHOLM

Telefon
växel 08-769 70 00

Telefon
direktval 08-769

Telex
19872 RPS STH S

Memorandum from Romander dated 18 February 1986, after the
visit to Baghdad of Mats Hellström

5

Terrorists and Traitors

When the ministers had assembled at nine o'clock on that first Saturday morning after the assassination, their immmediate priority was the appointment of a successor to the murdered premier. The veteran Sten Andersson, Minister of Foreign Affairs and former secretary of the Social Democratic Party, was approached, but he declined the post in favour of some younger man and, after a mere twenty-minute meeting, it was announced that the new prime minister, and by implication leader of the Social Democratic Party, would be Ingvar Carlsson, the former vice-premier.

Then they got down to the business of making the arrangements for Olof Palme's funeral, whose date they fixed for a fortnight later. They sent for Sven Åke Hjälmroth, head of SÄPO, and ordered him to work for Holmér to ensure the safety of all the participants and the efficient policing of the city.

'Gentlemen,' Hjälmroth said, 'you know that there is a killer at large, and if he is still at liberty in two weeks time, we are going to be faced with a security man's nightmare. Please, I implore you, don't make things worse by taking foolish risks yourselves. Any one of you might be the next target, so do not go anywhere, and I mean anywhere, without being escorted by your bodyguards.'

So, at the same time as the Swedish police forces were being mobilized in the most extensive manhunt in their history, they were faced with the greatest security operation which had ever confronted the country. Gösta Welander, Holmér's deputy, found himself largely responsible for the contribution of the Stockholm Police District force, due to the enormous demands on Holmér by the murder investigation. He followed with anxiety the frenetic activity of his chief and the Brains Trust, hoping and praying that Palme's killer would be safely behind bars before the funeral of Olof Palme on Saturday 15 March.

Unlike Holmér, who insisted on taking charge personally of the Brains Trust in its hunt for the killer, Welander deputed the security arrangements for the funeral and for the foreign visitors to a committee of regular, experienced policemen. As the list of distinguished but frequently controversial mourners lengthened, so did the faces of the men who were charged with their safety.

For Superintendent Sune Sandström, it was the challenge of his career. He knew he could call upon discreet assistance from SÄPO, and he was backed up from his own force by two chief detective inspectors, Werner Berggren and Sören Lindgren. The three of them were sitting in a small, sparsely furnished office, looking over the list of statesmen and other celebrities with a view to selecting those who might be considered extreme security risks.

Lindgren looked up and shook his head glumly. 'You know, if I had been told to pick the most likely targets in the whole world, I could not have done better than to duplicate these sheets.'

Sandström nodded. 'And we don't only have quality, but also quantity. How many of the bastards are there?'

'I haven't bothered to count,' replied Lindgren, 'there must be about 1,500, but whoever ran off these lists has pencilled in that there will be 120 states officially represented.'

Berggren pulled a crumpled piece of paper out of his pocket, smoothed it and turned to Sandström. 'I thought it might be interesting to check on how many terrorist attacks were committed in the ten years to the end of 1985,' he said. 'The total was 6,329 reported by police forces all over the world, and 2,379 of them were in Western Europe.'

'Gruesome,' commented his chief, 'but what's the point?'

'Well, as there is some outrage roughly every day and a half, just in our half of Europe, does it make sense trying to allocate priorities to targets? Surely every one of them is a target?'

'You can rely on Höglund to deal with bodyguards. I hear that SÄPO are running a crash course to train enough able-bodied men to act as temporary bodyguards. But let's not waste time sympathizing with them; we have enough problems of our own.'

'But still,' persisted Berggren, 'don't you see that, since there is such a universal epidemic of terrorism, it's on the cards that there might be some truly global conspiracy and that killing Palme was no more than the overture to something far more dramatic?'

The other two looked at him in silence.

'Just think for a moment what you would do if you were a true anarchist and wanted to get rid of the whole damned tribe of politicians. Shoot Palme, and you can be sure that the rest of them will swarm to the funeral. Then, one bloody great bomb would decimate them. No need to bother about individuals: they'll all be packed together at the funeral like sardines, won't they?'

Sandström sighed. 'No possibility can be excluded. However, we must also take precautions against more discriminating villains, don't you think? For example, I see that all three British parties are being represented by leading figures, Whitelaw for the Conservatives, Kinnock for Labour and Owen for the Alliance. Now wouldn't that be a mouth-watering prospect for an IRA marksman? And what about Mitterand? Can we afford not to take special precautions against an attempt by Action Directe? They've been very lively lately.'

Soberly they got down to the business of identifying the more obvious targets of groups who had been active recently. There were such men as Wilfried Martens, Prime Minister of Belgium, where the CCC (Cellules Communistes Combattantes) had carried off some spectacular *coups*. Could they count on none of the Italian organizations turning up to have a crack at Craxi, the Socialist premier, who was keeping together the precarious coalition which passed for a government? As for West Germany, providing both Chancellor Helmut Kohl and Foreign Minister Hans Dietrich Genscher, they were offering the Rote Arme Fraktione a double temptation, with Egon Bahr from the Bundestag and Willy Brandt thrown in as a bonus. And, to complicate matters, there were at least two other West German groups who might be ready to take up the challenge, Die Revolutionäre Zellen and Die Autonome.

Of course, the United States, whose delegation was to be headed by Secretary of State George Shultz, and the Soviet Union, represented by Prime Minister Ryshkov, were special cases. Although they would be bringing with them droves of their own Secret Service agents and all the latest in security gimmicks, Sandström knew that, if anything happened to members of either group, he would be in the hot seat.

A separate list was made of African leaders, such as Kenneth Kaunda of Zambia and Samora Machel from Mozambique, together with the South African anti-apartheid people, Archbishop Desmond Tutu and ANC chief Oliver Tambo in particular, who might attract the unwelcome attention of BOSS. As Sandström had said, no possibility could be excluded.

'Yoko Ono is among the American delegation,' said Lindgren. 'Remember when John Lennon was shot in New York?'

Sandström shook his head in irritation. 'Let's go through the whole damned list, name by name, and try to bring some sort of order into this. And don't forget that there are plenty of possible candidates for a bullet on the right as well as on the left.'

'I've been thinking,' Berggren announced. 'Is it right that the guests are going to be seated in alphabetical order of their countries during the ceremony?'

'Sure. It avoids any question of priority or protocol.'

'It means that Iran and Iraq will be next to each other,' said Berggren.

'Very awkward, but I hardly think that the official delegates will be assassins,' replied Sandström.

'You were the one who stressed that no possibility can be excluded,' said Berggren, in an aggrieved voice.

'I'm more concerned about the danger of UNITA having a go at the Angolan delegation, and almost anyone from Lebanon will have to be watched when Walid Jumblatt puts in an appearance.' Sandström began to tick off names from the list before him. 'And before either of you bothers to remind me, I *am* aware that Rajiv Gandhi is leading the Indian party and that his mother was killed by a Sikh fanatic.'

The announcement of the second detention of Gunnarsson on the Wednesday preceding the funeral did little to reassure them. Holmér was fully occupied with his mammoth investigation, and his extravagant demands on the manpower available aggravated the problems confronting his deputy, who saw himself being held responsible for ensuring the safety of the assembled world leaders. He willingly shared the burden with the SÄPO leaders, and Höglund, under the watchful eye of Hjälmroth, drew up the security plan, but the strain on the resources of the two simultaneous operations was colossal.

Their first ordeal was as George Shultz's plane came in to land and the police received an anonymous phone call that there was a bomb set to explode as it touched down. It proved to be a hoax.

The Grand Hotel was one of four chosen to accommodate the influx of VIPs. It is a luxurious establishment, reminiscent in its spaciousness and dignified furnishings of a bygone age, a combination of elegance and opulence. On the evening preceding the funeral, grave-faced politicians patronized the Franska Verandan (French Veranda), an exquisite restaurant on the right of the entrance lobby. The food was excellent, and the prices were sufficiently exalted to proclaim the importance of the diners, or the extent of their expense accounts. For those whose appetites were more modest, or whose public image was more humble, on the other side of the lobby were a bar and a less pretentious restaurant, which, however, deserved better than its popular name of 'the Poverty Veranda'.

While Asians puzzled over the complexities of *smörgåsbord*, Americans watched their waistlines, and tight-lipped men from Eastern Europe imbibed aquavit, members of the Swedish Ministry of Foreign Affairs flitted from one delegation to another, busy bees gathering the nectar of international small-talk. A small, wiry man wandered unobtrusively through the lobby, exchanging a nod or a few words: Anders Thunborg, a former Minister of Defence and one-time Swedish Ambassador to the United Nations, was on parade. Other men were even more inconspicuous. They talked to no one, but their eyes were ever watchful: SÄPO were also on parade. Other SÄPO men, carrying walkie-talkies, patrolled, three to each floor. Throughout the evening, more foreign guests arrived: the hotel had been completely taken over by official delegations. An unusual splash of colour among the sober-suited diplomats was provided by Jerry Rawlings, President of Ghana, who strode in, dressed in jungle combat uniform, complete with filled cartridge belt, flanked by a pair of similarly apparelled bodyguards.

Next day, the security operation went into top gear. Roads into the centre of the city were closed to all motor traffic, and a procession of dignified limousines carried the mourners from their hotels to the City Hall, where the formal ceremony was to take place. (It had been decided to hold a completely secular ceremony, since Palme was not a religious believer, so the police were at any rate spared the necessity of safeguarding a bevy of bishops.) As the cars wound their way through the crowded streets, one group of spectators waved Chilean flags. Chile and South Africa were the only countries of any importance not to send official representatives. It would have been too hypocritical a gesture, even for their Governments, to make a public show of mourning the man whom they had detested.

To their amazement, the statesmen, each one a living target, gazed out onto streets absolutely bereft of military uniforms. Not a soldier was to be seen, not a single sub-machine gun poked its snout out of the quiet, orderly throngs of civilians. Ingvar Carlsson had taken an immense gamble. He refused to call in the military, as being a betrayal of the values of democratic Sweden and of the late Prime Minister himself. This had been the wish of the Government, and the men from SÄPO and the Stockholm Police had agreed to go along with it.

'The eyes of the world are fixed on Sweden,' the new Prime Minister had stated to the police chiefs. 'It is up to you to demonstrate that we are still a civilized people who will not be panicked into adopting the trappings of force and imitating the men who live by the bullet and the bomb.'

It was a splendid affirmation of principle, but what would be the verdict of the world if there were to be another outrage, this time against a visiting statesman and in front of the television cameras? Already there had been some criticism at the apparent ease with which the assassin had walked away from the scene of his crime, but that had been muted when Holmér had triumphantly announced the detention, then the arrest, of his suspect.

There were a couple of moments of unforeseen crisis for the police. The PLO had sent an official delegation. It was one of Sandström's possibilities which could not be excluded that other Palestinians or their sympathizers might have arrived in Sweden to settle their account with Shimon Peres, Prime Minister of Israel. Sandström was appalled, therefore, when Peres refused to accept the place reserved for him in one of the limousines. Since the funeral was taking place on a Saturday, the Jewish Sabbath, and orthodox Jews regard riding as an infraction of the rules for the observance of the Sabbath, the Prime Minister insisted in walking from the Grand Hotel to the City Hall.

'I didn't know that Peres was so orthodox,' complained Sandström.

'Maybe he isn't, but a hell of a lot of Israeli voters are,' rejoined Höglund.

It was an enormous relief when the procession reached the City Hall without any incident, and the simple ceremony was completed. A young woman spoke on behalf of the Social Democratic youth and the young people of the whole country, a Finnish woman sang *'Gracias a la Vida'* in a special Swedish translation, and the main oration was delivered by Willy Brandt. At last, the children's choir had sung their final tribute, the final strains of solemn music had died away and the participants were spirited away.

The cortège, led by a troop of soldiers beating muffled drums, moved slowly through the centre of Stockholm, bearing the coffin to the Adolf Fredriks churchyard, barely a hundred metres from where Palme had been shot down. Here, only members of the family were permitted to enter the cemetery: the final farewell to Olof Palme was a poignant, intimate affair. Only then were Lisbeth Palme, her sons and their relations permitted to grieve in decent privacy.

The speeches had been made, the simple song had echoed away and the mourners had departed. Once more the streets were open. Then Erich Honecker decided that he would pay a personal tribute to the memory of the fallen Socialist by making a pilgrimage to the spot where he had been gunned down. Tass had immediately condemned the murder as the work of American imperialists, and members of the Supreme Soviet stood in silence for a minute, an honour which they had not paid to President Kennedy. Peres had got away with his promenade: would the East German leader be so fortunate? The police chiefs waited in tense silence for the reports from their men on the spot.

But even when every man and woman had been delivered safely back to their hotels, the ordeal for the police was not by any means over. Not all the visitors emulated François Mitterand, who arrived at the last moment in a private plane and left the instant the ceremony was completed, pleading the pressure of work. The gathering in Stockholm gave an opportunity for informal, discreet conversations between men who could not normally meet without attracting widespread attention and speculation, such as Shultz and Ryshkov, Kohl and Honecker. And in the evening there was the formal reception organized by the Ministry of Foreign Affairs at the Arvfurstens Palats in the Gustav Adolfs Torg, to which all the foreign delegations were invited. Every practical precaution had been taken, although without any fuss. All the police chiefs could do now was to wait and watch – and pray that their measures would prove to be sufficient to cope with any incident which might occur. When, finally, the last VIP had made his farewells and nothing had shattered the surface calm of the obsequies and the meetings, the relief of Sandström and his men was almost tangible. Now they could get back to the everyday tasks of policing a great city and finding the murderer of their premier.

While the funeral was in progress, and the delegations had departed from the Grand Hotel, leaving the lobby and the restaurants strangely deserted, a less exalted meeting was taking place. In the bar, a couple of solitary drinkers talked quietly. One was a middle-aged man who was sometimes known as Birger Trovald, ostensibly an import-export agent but actually a senior member of the Counter-Espionage Department of the Security Police. Of course, although his car was registered in the name of Birger Trovald and that was what appeared in the telephone directory and the commercial register, neither his parents nor his wife had any idea of the identity of a person of that name. Trovald had made being unobtrusive into an art. He habitually assumed the anxious expression of a clergyman who has become aware that he has left his umbrella on a bus, although in the presence of his close friends he dropped the mask and reverted to his natural bluff and hearty self. He carried with him the meerschaum pipe which he had bought in London, where he had been involved in talks with members of MI5. As he explained, the pipe was no more than a talisman, since Trovald was a non-smoker, but it was a necessary accoutrement for one who aspired to emulate Sherlock Holmes. 'Who knows?' he would say. 'If I rub it like Aladdin's lamp, the genie of brother Mycroft might rise up before me and show me how to solve some baffling problem.'

The man who sat opposite him was one of the few who knew the real nature of his work. There had been an occasion when he had been tentatively approached by a pleasant young man who had suggested that Erik Johansson, as a trusted official of the Department of Foreign Trade in the Ministry of Foreign Affairs, might come across some documents which could conceivably be of interest to the well-intentioned men in the Kremlin. Of course, they would not dream of asking him to reveal anything which might be damaging to his country, that would be treasonable, and they were honest, law-abiding citizens of the world. Nevertheless, if Johansson, without tormenting his conscience, were able to pass on some harmless scraps of information, his complaisance would not go unrewarded. Johansson, slightly bald and rather overweight, had a pink, cherubic countenance and the eager eyes of a schoolboy, but he deported himself with the propriety expected of a civil servant of some standing. When he was invited to indulge in a spot of inoffensive espionage, he expressed some misgivings but allowed himself to be flattered and persuaded – and immediately reported the contact to SÄPO. He was requested to play along, and Trovald was assigned to liaise with him and provide him with some tasty morsels of gossip and misinformation which he duly passed on. Eventually, Johansson's comrades either guessed that they were being duped or decided that the quality of his reports was not of a sufficiently high standard to warrant keeping him on their books. The quiet chats over a coffee or a drink suddenly stopped, but the friendship between him and Trovald remained, based on mutual trust and respect for each other's shrewdness.

'So what do you boys make of this man Holmér has arrested?' asked Johansson.

'Pure bullshit,' Trovald laughed. 'We've done our homework on the EAP, and I promise you that Holmér is barking up the wrong tree. Not that they are an appetizing bunch, mind you.'

'I don't know anything about them. How did they come to crawl out of the woodwork?'

'Well, it's not exactly what I would call a mass movement. I suppose their office employs ten or twelve staff, and that's more than the total membership of the party. Of course, they've tried to get support through all their cover organizations, but the whole outfit is a tiny handful of thugs, even if we include the office cat.'

'Are you saying they're not dangerous?' challenged Johansson.

'One man is dangerous if he's crazy and has a gun,' answered Trovald, 'but get out of your head any idea of some great

underground revolutionary force, poised to overthrow democracy, capitalism or society in general.'

'Yet they run an office and they put out literature, don't they?
If they have practically no members, where do they get the
money from to keep going?'

'That's a good question, and one the police are looking at,'
said Trovald with an approving smile. 'There are suggestions
that, when it was founded, the CIA put up the cash.'

'You are not suggesting that it was the CIA who killed Palme?'
asked Johansson incredulously.

Trovald shook his head. 'I wouldn't put it past them, but I
don't think it's likely. And I'm pretty sure they've stopped
giving a helping hand to the EAP, which has been putting out
some virulently anti-American propaganda – despite the fact
that the man behind it is himself an American.'

'So why was the CIA financing a revolutionary workers'
movement?'

'Because it was not truly revolutionary and had nothing to do
with workers. This man, Lyndon La Rouche, who joined the
Trotskyist Socialist Workers' Party in the United States back in
1949, was actually a wealthy businessman, but as a student he'd
made a study of Marxism and philosophy in general. He quit
soon afterwards to form his own group, the International
Campus of Labour Committees.'

'What's all this got to do with Sweden?' demanded
Johansson.

'Well, you see, there was a whole brood of European offshoots
known as the European Labour Committees, but here in
Sweden the group was called the European Workers' Party.
Back in the seventies, a lot of people in the States were worried
at what they saw as a growing movement towards radicalism in
Europe, what with the earlier student unrest, the revolution in
Portugal and above all the opposition to American action in
Vietnam. They realized that the European Labour Committees
were simply hot-air talking-shops which could be used to attract
muddle-headed young leftists away from genuine militant
parties. La Rouche married a German, Helga Zepp, and set up
his headquarters in Wiesbaden, very handy for important
American overt and covert establishments.'

'And in Sweden?'

'The EAP attacked Palme as being a capitalist pawn and, at the same time, a Soviet agent. They went so far as to claim that they were the sole legitimate heirs of the First Socialist International, the one Marx set up in London in 1864, because a group had gone to the States in 1872, despite the fact that the International had been formally dissolved and its organization in the States liquidated.'

'And the police are concentrating on that bunch of weirdos?' asked Johansson incredulously.

'That's the way it is,' assented his friend with a wry smile.

'And SÄPO?'

'We have our own ideas. Let's say we're looking closer to home.'

'I'd be tempted to look further overseas,' countered Erik Johansson.

'Of course, we're watching foreign agents, the comrades and the cousins. But which of the secret armies did you have in mind?'

'How about Iraq? It was only a month or two ago that the papers were full of that murder by their hit-men.'

'One hit-man and one hit-woman that we know of.' There was no mirth in Birger Trovald's smile. 'Sure, they killed Majed Husain, but what reason would they have for hostility towards Sweden?'

'Have a look at the trade statistics. Despite Sweden's loudly proclaimed neutrality, trade with Iran and Iraq is of considerable importance, even according to the official figures, and they obviously don't take any account of goods which end up in either country after having been exported to some other place, such as Singapore. But look at the way we've switched the emphasis of our exports from Iraq to Iran. Don't you think that would get the Iraqis annoyed?'

'I can't say I ever paid any attention to that. Do you have the figures?'

Johansson grinned delightedly. 'I hoped you might ask: I brought them along on purpose. Hang on a moment.' He rummaged in his pockets and produced a scrap of paper. 'Now listen to this. Up to the end of 1982, Swedish shipments to Iraq were much bigger than those to Iran. Exports to Iraq rose from 2,908 million kronor in 1981 to 2,961 million in 1982, whereas those to Iran only went from 998 million to 1,293 million. But in the following year there was a huge switching of Swedish trade, exports to Iraq falling to 1,029 million kronor whereas those to Iran soared to 3,233 million kronor. Do you realize that by then Iran was taking more goods from Sweden than the USSR, with 2,228 million kronor?'

'Interesting,' Trovald conceded, 'but hardly a reason to murder the Prime Minister.'

'Dig around,' Johansson advised. 'It's simply a hunch I have at this time, but you should be able to see if there are other factors which would strengthen the case. You have to admit they are brutal enough to kill anyone if it appeared to be in their interest.'

'That's true enough. But that's not the direction in which we're looking. Here, let me get you another drink.'

As Birger Trovald walked across to the bar, he reflected that Erik Johansson was no fool: maybe his hunch would be worth closer examination, when he had time.

The Iraqi Embassy is at 6A Baldersgatan, not far from the complex of buildings which comprise Radio House. The ambassador, His Excellency Mohammed Said Kadhim Al-Sahaf, had just received a verbal report from Salam Noufan Abid, officially the second secretary to the embassy, in fact the intelligence officer. He in turn had checked with the attachés Ibrahim Ali Mendil, Salah Shatab, Hamdi Abid Ibrahim and Mohammed Abbas, whose duties, also unofficially, encompassed security. The 'diplomats' were satisfied: there had been no suggestion in the Swedish media that they or their colleagues had been involved in the assassination of Olof Palme. There had been nothing like the blatant disregard of Swedish susceptibilities shown by the executioners of Majed Husain. Things were working out exactly as they had hoped. The police forces of their host country were fully occupied.

A taxi drew up a few blocks from the embassy, but its occupants walked away across the parking lot and into the reception area of Radio House and went into the cafeteria which stands on the left side of the entrance hall. Ruth had returned with the Olssons to Stockholm with a few bruises as souvenirs of the ski slopes but with her limbs unbroken. Sven was waiting for them at a table with coffee, pastries and all the latest news and gossip. He kissed Ruth and then turned to greet her aunt and uncle.

'You must have heard about the resignation of Karl Svensson as public prosecutor in the Palme enquiry,' he said.

'Yes,' growled Lars Olsson. 'Good riddance! It's a damned scandal the way he obstructed the police. Now he's out of the way, we might see some real action.'

Sven grinned. 'I see that you have been reading Holmér's account of what went on. Do you know that Svensson went to the Attorney General to complain about improper use of confrontations of the man who had been detained by witnesses?'

'No.'

'It hasn't been in the papers,' said the young reporter. He was obviously pleased at being able to display his inside knowledge in front of Ruth.

'Well, it doesn't change my opinion,' retorted Lars. 'And it doesn't seem to be sufficient reason for the man to withdraw from the case like some blasted prima donna.'

'Oh, there was more to it than that. Svensson is not a man to go out to get publicity, but Holmér made so many remarks in both public and private that, for I think the first time in his life, Svensson issued a press release. He stated quite baldly that there was no credible evidence against the man and that, if he had taken the case into court, he would have been made to look ridiculous, and so would the police and the whole of Swedish justice.'

'Well, I suppose that's the last we shall hear about that suspect, but there are plenty more of those EAP creeps about. Perhaps Holmér will be able to nail another one, and the new prosecutor, whoever he may be, won't be quite as squeamish as Svensson,' said Lars.

'The new man is Claes Zeime. He's the senior public prosecutor in the city, Svensson's boss, in point of fact. But I don't think we've heard the last of this suspect. Since he was named in a provincial newspaper and his photograph published, I have a shrewd suspicion he'll claim damages both from the state and from the paper,' answered Sven. 'As for Holmér, he seems determined to concentrate on the EAP people in spite of his failure to nail Gunnarsson.'

However, Sven was doing less than justice to Holmér's line of investigation. The police chief was convinced that the culprit was crazy, but he did not confine himself to the EAP, now that he had been obliged to concede defeat over Gunnarsson. In fact, the EAP trail soon died out. With the first onslaught on them, the leaders had made themselves scarce, but as they slowly re-emerged, they found themselves faced with an unexpected problem. Since they had concentrated their venom against Palme, his death had left them without any obvious alternative target. They relapsed into silence, and by the middle of April even Holmér had consigned them into the 'dead duck' category.

Holmér was left with two alternatives, both of which he pursued. Either the killer was an individual, a Swede who would eventually give himself away, the theory which he had been nursing even before he had got back to Stockholm on the morning of 1 March to take control of the case, or he was a member of one of the foreign terrorist organizations which from time to time disrupt normal life by committing some atrocity.

Efforts to glean information from the public were stepped up, and at the end of March a reward of 500,000 kronor was offered, a measure which required Holmér's obtaining a legal and financial approval by the Government. The telephone calls on the 'hot line' poured in. Between March and May alone, no fewer than 45,000 were received, not one of which proved to be of the slightest practical value. Computerized lists were compiled of everyone who had ever claimed to be a victim of some miscarriage of justice, real or imaginary, and there was apparently no limit to the extent of the police sniffing into lonely eccentrics, possible public enemies, self-styled political parties, dissidents, known grumblers, trouble-makers and individuals noted for their cussedness or cantankerous attitude. No matter how far-fetched the allegation, no one escaped scrutiny.

Holmér himself actively pushed ahead with developing his alternative theory, rooting out dangerous terrorists from overseas who had infected Swedish society.

'What have we got on that mob who hijacked an Aeroflot airliner?' he asked. 'When was that?'

'February 1979,' replied Linder. 'But you're wasting your time. Ananda Marga, as they call themselves, are really a spent force. You remember their guru, don't you, Shri Shri Anandamurti? His real name was Prabat Ranjan Sarkar, and he was some sort of glorified clerk with Indian Railways.'

'Yes, but they got up to a lot of mischief, didn't they?'

'Usually against Indian diplomats. Mind you, they killed that guy, Biswanatan Singh, and dumped his body in a sack into a lake between Stockholm and Norrtälje. Seems that he'd been a member of their precious sect and had defected.'

'Sounds a bit like those Iraqis last year,' remarked someone, but no one paid any attention.

'We've checked on their propaganda. It's the usual lunatic confusion – a spot of Marxism mixed up with Buddhism, Hinduism and doses of yoga and meditation.'

'Meditation!' snorted Holmér. 'They seem to practise a rather violent form of meditation.'

'Yes,' Linder agreed, 'but there's no record of their ever having aired any grievance against Palme, or the Social Democrats. For years, their support has been dwindling. I don't think we should give high priority to following them up. Now, the Kurds, they are a different matter.'

'I thought you might be going to tell me that they only kill Turks,' Holmér sneered facetiously.

'Sure, Turks are their prime targets,' Linder said patiently. 'but unlike Ananda Marga they are still active, and they have attacked Palme, verbally at any rate.'

Holmér nodded. 'Yes, I remember. Let's concentrate on what those villains have been up to. Get your men onto it. And let me have the file on the Kurdistan Workers' Party: I'll go over it carefully this evening.'

And that was how the main effort of the police shifted away from the European Workers Party to the militant Kurds. No one suggested turning to the Iraqis. Salam Noufan Abid had good reason to be contented.

One man who was far from contented was Karl Svensson. He had withdrawn from the case not in a fit of pique but out of a profound conviction that the police inquiry was being run on entirely the wrong lines. He had agonized before issuing his statement to the press, and he was anxious to get something positive done. So he visited Police Headquarters, where Holmér was holding court, but he went to one of the upper floors, which was occupied by SÄPO. He expressed his deep concern to Superintendent Kent Robért.

'While this Brains Trust of Holmér's rushes after every red herring, its great stuff for the TV cameras, but the real criminal is getting more and more elusive. Can't SÄPO do something about it?'

Robért was sympathetic but unhelpful. He pointed out that the Government was backing the Stockholm Police District's handling of the investigation and that SÄPO had no brief to interfere.

'We've offered our advice and assistance,' he said, 'but they've been refused. We can't force the boys downstairs to take them. I'm afraid there's nothing that we can do now apart from waiting for Holmér to bash his head against a brick wall of his own making. Only when he is brought to realize that his methods are not paying off will we get our chance.'

Sadly Svensson took his leave: Robért watched him go. He had been less than frank with the public prosecutor: people in SÄPO were already involved in their own parallel and strictly unofficial investigation. While the force would respond to any request that might be made to them, it was vital that their own burrowing away after the truth be shielded from interference by Holmér or any parliamentary committee which might be set up. Quietly, away from all the publicity, facts were being brought together and deductions formed, but months of dogged work would be necessary before they could hope for any results.

The official headquarters of SÄPO are two of the upper floors of the complex occupied by the National Police, a building which also houses the Stockholm Police District. It is a place which can easily be kept under observation, so it is not surprising that much of the work of the Security Police is carried out in back rooms of unassuming shops or offices in some of the dingier districts of the capital. For instance, if you were to enter the premises of Wesyls Handels AB, you could experience some difficulty in carrying through a conventional trading operation. If, however, your commodity was information, it might be that you would be ushered into a back room in which stood a battered wooden desk, a row of second-hand steel filing-cabinets (or that is what they looked like) and a bookcase containing several trade journals and reference books. The layer of dust on the plain green lampshade might give the impression of having been installed with the fixtures and fittings, as would the clumsy, old-fashioned black telephone. Seated at the desk, you would meet a rather thick-set man in his early fifties with dark, beetling eyebrows and a bushy mane of grizzled hair, but gentle, trusting eyes, the sort of man who could well have spent a lifetime arranging shipments of vegetable oil or scrap iron, poring over bills of lading and certificates of insurance and contacting banks to argue about amendments to the clauses of a letter of credit. Birger Trovald really looked the part of a plodding, uninspired but reliable shipping clerk.

Whereas the official investigation was fastening on foreign terrorists, the favoured SÄPO approach was to look into cases of Swedish nationals who had been guilty of subversion. Trovald, as part of the operation, was very systematically working through the files of known spies. Other men and women were checking on the activities of foreign espionage organizations, but since no exceptional radio activity had been detected around the time of the assassination by the military radio surveillance unit (FRA – Försvarets Radioanstalt), more emphasis was being put on sniffing out home-grown traitors.

Sweden's ace mole had been Stig Wennerström, an air force colonel who later became military attaché at the embassy in Washington. Back in Stockholm, Wennerström had been appointed to the Disarmament Division of the Ministry of Foreign Affairs. His traffic in secret information had been sufficiently valuable to earn him the rank of general in the Red Army. The fact that the top floor of his villa contained extensive radio equipment had aroused the suspicions of the woman who cleaned his house, but for years she kept them to herself. Eventually, SÄPO too began to have some doubts about the probity of the colonel, and when they questioned the woman, the truth about Wennerström soon emerged. The cleaning woman explained that she had wanted to inform SÄPO long before the master spy was unmasked, but she had been unable to find them in the telephone directory. The results of the affair were that Wennerström was sentenced to life imprisonment in 1962 (but pardoned in the mid seventies) and that the secret police are now listed as RIKSPOLISSTYRELSEN/Säkerhetsav- delningen and their number as 769 7000: there is a twenty-four-hour telephone service in case another cleaning woman happens to find herself being asked to dust an illicit transmitter.

Even within the ranks of SÄPO itself, a case had been discovered of information being sold to the Soviet Union. The net closed around Detective Inspector Stig Bergling, who was SÄPO's man in charge of liaison with Military Intelligence.

Bergling fled to the Soviet Union but chose a roundabout route to throw pursuers off the scent. However, he made the mistake of going via Israel, where men from MOSSAD arrested him on the spot and, without waiting for the formalities of extradition proceedings, sent him straight back to Sweden. He was sentenced to life imprisonment, but his subsequent escape and flight to the Soviet Union were to prove a further embarrassment to the Swedish authorities.

Colonel Ströberg, serving on the Army General Staff, proved even more inept. He wrote to the Polish Embassy, proposing to deliver secrets against payment and enclosing a few samples for approval. Not unnaturally, the Poles did not believe that so blatant an offer could be anything other than a cunning, capitalist provocation. They handed over the good colonel's correspondence to the Ministry of Foreign Affairs, protesting that the People's Republic of Poland did not indulge in such underhand practices as espionage, although their overseas representatives were required to exercise 'socialist watchfulness'. When Colonel Ströberg strolled into the post office to collect the letter which should have been waiting for him under an assumed name, he was greeted by a reception committee from SÄPO.

Birger Trovald frowned and ploughed on through the records. There was just one other case of a Swedish national, again a member of the intelligence community who had been convicted as a spy, working for the USSR during the sixties. He opened the file of Chief Detective Inspector Hans Melin of the Aliens Department of the Stockholm Police District, who had sold information on refugees to the Soviet Union and was then arrested in his apartment in Sveavägen in the company of an agent of the Iraqi intelligence service.

Trovald put down the file and considered. All these stale cases of selling secrets to the Soviet Union or its satellites petered out in dead ends – the same pattern was repeated each time. But now he was presented with a fresh avenue. Iraq had meddled in Sweden before: was it conceivable that it was implicated in the death of Palme? He was brought back to Johansson's hunch.

Other SÄPO officers noted grimly that since 1960 every single Swedish national who had been convicted for espionage had been a member of the armed forces or a police officer. They started looking closely for suspects in the Palme case within their own ranks.

Some years previously there had been a public outcry over the alleged brutality of a group of policemen at Norrmalms police station, which is located within the Stockholm Police District. Their area included the Central Railway Station, from which they were expected to expel drunks, dope-pushers and dossers. Although the police had been cleared of causing the death of an old man who had been taken into custody, they were labelled by their critics in the press as 'the Baseball Gang', since it was stated that they had used baseball bats excessively in the execution of their duties. The discovery that one of the Baseball Gang had been close to the spot where Palme was murdered on that Friday night was sufficient reason for his flat to be searched, but the man had an alibi, and nothing incriminating was found. There were a number of other examples of police who had appeared at some time or other to be unduly zealous and whose conduct had caused alarm, even though they had been exonerated of any actual crime, but none of these could be credibly connected with the murder. However, over a period of ten months, some twenty officers of the National Police Force were tactfully assigned to other duties. If SÄPO had been no more successful than Holmér in unmasking the killer of Olof Palme, they had at least achieved something positive in their close scrutiny of the ranks of the police and security forces.

SÄPO were not the only people who had decided to follow up their own hunch. Ever since Holmér's ill-tempered outburst after the release of Gunnarsson by Svensson, he had lost the confidence of a large section of the press which had previously accepted without question his confident predictions of a rapid resolution of the case. Their growing doubts if anything stimulated the police chief to even stronger affirmations of his theories and yet more sweeping claims.

Sven Beckman listened to the acid comments of older and more experienced journalists and decided to carry out a little research on his own account. The timing of this initiative was unfortunate, since it coincided with Ruth's preparations for her return to Britain, and she could not help feeling that a live girlfriend should have a stronger claim on the young man's attention and the limited time left for them together than a dead prime minister.

Her sightseeing in the historic part of the city had taken Ruth to the splendid Riddarhuset, the House of the Knights, but Sven was too busy to accompany her. She met her aunt for lunch at the nearby Restaurant Cattelin, where she sampled the halibut and washed it down with Skåne, a strong yellowish aquavit which did little to mellow her mood towards Sven who was too tied up to join them. Eventually he took her for a beer at The Pub, a busy meeting-place inside the Central Station, not the most romantic setting but practical, Sven assured her, if one was pressed for time.

'I think one has to dig into Palme's past to see if there were people who had personal rather than political reasons for hating the man,' he confided, 'and I have come up with a first-class scandal. I believe he was a party to a big cover-up and that he lied to the press.'

'That sounds like everyday politics,' replied Ruth.

'Don't be so cynical.' Sven resented her offhand dismissal of his revelations.

'I suppose your little Lena has been helping you with your detective work,' Ruth said.

'Well, yes, as a matter of fact, she has been useful in going through some of the records for me.'

'She seems to be taking up a lot of your time,' Ruth observed bitterly.

Sven stared at her. 'I think you're jealous,' he accused.

Ruth got to her feet. 'I must be getting back,' she said. 'And I wouldn't want to keep you away from your research, or whatever it is that you get up to all day long.'

Sven felt a wave of anger at what he considered her unreasonableness. He wanted to stop her leaving in a bad temper and to find his way back into the warm glow of her affection, but his stubborn pride and conviction that she was the one who ought to make up their silly tiff held him back. The best he could manage was to call out to her that he would phone her.

'Don't bother,' she called without looking back.

Damn her, Sven seethed. When he came up with a real scoop, she'd be sorry she'd been so petty. He visualized her pleading for his forgiveness, as he made his way to meet Lena.

What had caught Sven's imagination was the series of events which Holmér had dismissed as 'the Persson business'. Karl Persson was the founder of the Swedish National Police; previously the regional forces had all been autonomous. As

Secretary of State at the Ministry of the Interior, he had created a system which brought together all the local forces, as well as SÄPO, under the jurisdiction of a national organization, and in 1965 he became the first Director General of the National Police. Karl Persson was an austere man, strong willed and uncompromising in his pursuit of justice and hunting down of transgressors, regardless of their social position or political prestige. It was unfortunate for him that he came into collision with the Minister of Justice, Lennart Geijer.

The Social Democrats had been dogged with bad luck with their Ministers of Justice. One had committed suicide, and his successor had to be shifted because he was too conservative, but he fitted in nicely in his new appointment as ambassador to Copenhagen. Then came Geijer, able and with a sense of social purpose.

The two men were natural antagonists. Persson was a strict authoritarian who had constructed an efficient machine for combating crime. His view of criminals was unsentimental: if men and women committed acts which were condemned by society, they were to be caught and punished. Geijer saw them as victims of the injustice and heartlessness of that very society; they were the underprivileged, and their judges, respectable and respected, were the representatives of an over-privileged class. Whereas Persson restricted his aim to tracking down criminals, Geijer strove to change society.

What brought this uneasy relationship to breaking-point was an apparently trivial incident. A young woman was detained and brought into the headquarters of the Stockholm Police District on suspicion of being involved in a narcotics offence. She was searched, and a detective, leafing through her address book, came across Lennart Geijer's name.

'Do you know this man?' asked the policeman.

'Sure, he's my boyfriend,' she replied.

'Yeah, and my girlfriend is the Queen of England,' jeered the detective.

But the woman stuck to her statement: it was reported to the detective's superior officer and eventually to the head of the anti-drugs squad. He wanted to avoid any unpleasantness, so he sent a couple of his men to try to persuade the woman to amend her story. A short, sharp interview ought to have done the trick, but she refused to be intimidated by the forces of law and order, and the detectives were reluctantly obliged to accept that she was telling the truth. This put the head of the anti-drugs squad on the spot, so he took the logical course. He passed the report on to someone else who would then have to take the responsibility. That someone was Karl Persson.

This was a serious matter. The Chief of the National Police handed the dossier to Olof Palme himself and stated that, in his opinion, the Minister of Justice was a security risk. However, it was obvious that Palme did not share his concern. Persson's report was filed away and quietly forgotten. But it was not forgotten by Persson himself: he let Geijer know of the file that existed on him and when, from time to time, the police chief wanted to exert a little gentle pressure on the minister, the mention of it ensured that Geijer did not prove troublesome.

Then, on 20 August 1976, Persson requested an urgent meeting with Palme. A general election was pending and what Persson had unearthed could be political dynamite. For some time the police had been looking into the activities of a forty-six-year-old woman who was running an agency for prostitutes – while prostitution itself is not a crime in Sweden, living off the earnings of whores is. The police had swooped and taken away the woman's address books and other records. That was how they found that among her clients was Thorbjörn Fälldin, the leader of the opposition party in Parliament and Palme's rival. Persson knew what a scandal disclosure of this could cause, and the effect it would have on Fälldin's prospects: he handed to Palme this key to an election victory. To his consternation, Palme refused to use it. He told Persson that he did not resort to dirty tricks and that he would win at the polls by fair means. His policies would be accepted by the Swedish people in preference to anything which the opposition might offer – and, anyhow, Swedes always elected Social Democratic Governments.

Karl Persson was frustrated and annoyed, but worse was to come. Against Palme's confident predictions, the Swedes voted for a change. He was out of power, and the new Prime Minister was Fälldin. The police chief understood that, as soon as Fälldin was in office, Palme had handed him Persson's report, containing his name. Drastic action was needed to forestall the new Prime Minister, and Persson decided to leak his report. He took it to Holmér, then head of SÄPO, but Holmér followed

Palme's lead and declined to have anything to do with it. So Persson persuaded the head of the counter-espionage division, Olof Frånstedt, to do his dirty work.

The outcome was not what Persson had predicted. The story which appeared in *Dagens Nyheter*, the highest-circulation morning paper in the country, in November 1977, accused Geijer, as former Minister of Justice, of suppressing the report and thus condoning the prostitution racket. Palme could no longer remain silent. He wrote a letter which the paper published, denying that there was any truth or substance in the story. Geijer threatened to sue, and the newspaper was forced to retract. In an out-of-court settlement, Geijer was paid 50,000 kronor, which he magnanimously handed over to a fund to be used to promote investigative journalism. The scandal was raised in Parliament, where members of all parties agreed that Persson's report was sheer nonsense, and a short time later Persson and Frånstedt were given every assistance by the Government Chancery in the preparation of their applications for new jobs, minor appointments in remote areas. Holmér was rewarded for his virtuous refusal to become involved by being promoted to head the Stockholm Police District.

In an effort to salvage his reputation, Persson complained to the Chancellor of Justice, who agreed to make a judicial enquiry. He concluded that Persson had been fully justified in handing this sensitive and controversial report to Palme. But that was all the satisfaction which Karl Persson obtained before he went into retirement.

Sven had no difficulty in finding out that Persson was still active as a security consultant. Surely here was a man with a strong and justified grudge against Palme and, with his expertise in police organization and security matters, he would possess the ability to mount an assassination which would be executed professionally and effectively. Sven resolved to raise the matter with one of the prosecutors, indirectly and informally, through the good offices of Lena. Svensson's approach to SÄPO had become known to Lena, among others in the office, and Sven urged her to present his hypothesis to her boss.

Lena shook her head. 'Sorry, darling, but that's not on. I don't mind passing on to you anything I happen to hear, provided it doesn't land me in any trouble, but you don't know Svensson.

He's one of the old school, very correct. It would be more than my job is worth to go to him with this notion of yours.'

'But don't you see how important this could be?'

Lena took a more light-hearted approach to life than Sven, but she could see how much it meant to the reporter to be able to test his pet theory on someone with greater experience than himself.

'I tell you what,' she said. 'This SÄPO man my boss knows, I've been able to have a few words with him, and he seems a nice enough guy. Why don't I chat him up a bit and tell him what you suspect?'

'Who is he?' Sven demanded.

'That's none of your business,' teased Lena. 'But he's not bad looking, quite smashing really.'

Sven suppressed his annoyance. A newsman has to sacrifice his personal feelings in the call of duty. Actually, Lena went and talked to one of the junior prosecutors, but she thought it amusing to keep up the pretence. A few days later, she called Sven.

'My boyfriend in SÄPO says I should tell you not to watch so many movies. He has met Persson and says he's too old to entertain ambitions which would drive him to remove a man who could stand in his way. More important, he's a fanatical supporter of the rule of law, the last man who would resort to an act of crude terrorism or barbaric revenge. They were his exact words.'

Lena relayed the prosecutor's opinion to Sven with a certain amount of amusement. 'Then he asked me out to dinner,' she said with a broad grin. 'I got the impression that he rather fancied me.'

Sven scowled. What with Ruth's bad temper and now Lena's flightiness, he was fast going off women.

'I thought I'd give him a bit of encouragement, and now we're going steady,' Lena smirked. 'After all, SÄPO are following up leads of their own; you never know, he might pass on some bit of information which you could use in a story. If you like, I'll introduce you some day.'

Sven sniffed disdainfully. He had been snubbed and slighted by some whipper-snapper of a cop: it was hardly likely that such a guy would prove to be the source for a sensational scoop.

*

Whatever his shortcomings, no one could accuse Hans Holmér of lack of enthusiasm. He became immersed in his study of the file on the evil-doings of the Kurdistan Workers Party, and the more he looked into the organization, the more convinced he was that now at last he was on the track of the gang which had killed Palme.

Partiya Karkaren Kurdistan, generally known by its initials, PKK, or the translation of its name into Swedish, Kurdiska Arbetarpartiet, had a record of violence in many European countries. As Linder had stated, it concentrated on attacks on Turkish diplomats, but not to the total exclusion of other victims. It had murdered individuals who were known to be sympathetic to the Turks, and there had also been a number of members of the organization who had wanted to get out and who were assisted by PKK to make sure that their departure was irreversible. Would-be defectors had been killed in West Germany, the Netherlands, Denmark and Switzerland.

In Sweden, there had already been two 'incidents'. In the summer of 1984 Enver Ata had been killed at Uppsala, and in November the following year Cetin Güngör had been despatched in Stockholm itself, at the busy Medborgarplatsen. There was no doubt, therefore, that the PKK qualified as a prime suspect if the criterion was simply willingness to shed blood without compunction or remorse.

But what about a motive? In general terms, its leader, Abdulla Özalan, or 'Apo' as he was usually styled, claimed that the party was a guerrilla movement on Marxist-Leninist lines. More relevant was the fact that it had a specific grievance against the Swedish Government. In December 1984 nine PKK members were detained in Stockholm, and the PKK itself was declared to be a terrorist organization. As was normal practice in such circumstances, the expulsion of the nine detainees was ordered by the Government, under the provisions of the controversial Terrorist Law. But this decision presented the authorities with a dilemma. There is no death penalty in Sweden, and it is against the law to deport anyone from Sweden to a country where they may face a death sentence. This certainly would have applied if the nine were shipped off to Turkey, and no other country was willing to extend a welcome to them. So, while it was illegal for them to reside in Sweden, it was also illegal to expel them. The Government ruled that they should stay but be confined to the

municipalities where they lived. This might not be regarded as a
particularly harsh condition, but it stirred up vehement protests
from some lawyers and well-meaning liberals, as well as from
the Kurds themselves. The nine had not been tried and
convicted of any specific offence, so it was argued that they
should be either prosecuted or released unconditionally.
Holmér noted with grim satisfaction that Olof Palme himself
was the target for the most bitter of these attacks: the Kurds
were not the sort of people, in his judgement, to limit their
onslaught to words alone.

The main thrust of the investigation was now concentrated on
the PKK, and Holmér made no secret of it. His failure with the
EAP had not made him any less ready to stick out his neck with
the media. Throughout April and May, he repeatedly asserted
his certainty that the PKK were guilty, although, as time passed
without any definite arrest, he qualified his statements more
frequently with the admission that he did not yet possess proof
of their guilt which would stand up in court.

Holmér's confidence was not shared universally by his
colleagues in the National Police. There was a feeling that he
was preparing a position on which he could retreat if he drew a
blank with the PKK, as he had with the EAP. He could then
retire from the case with honour: he had pinned responsibility
where it belonged; it was not his fault if the snags of legal
technicalities had prevented him from bringing the culprits to
their just punishment. This would leave his successor with an
unenviable task, but that would no longer be a consideration for
Holmér himself, who could then devote his energies to yet more
urgent matters.

The quiet men in SÄPO had never accepted Holmér's
assessment of the PKK. While no one would dispute their
capability or their motive, ill-judged though it may have been,
there were important considerations which appeared to
exonerate them from this specific atrocity. If they had avenged
themselves on Palme, why had they not proclaimed the fact? It
was logical to expect that they would have trumpeted it from the
rooftops, but there had not been as much as a whisper. Then
again, when the PKK committed 'executions', there had never
been any problem in finding the killers. Their methods were
open, and the killers disdained attempting to escape: the style of
Palme's murder did not bear their stamp. And the final

argument was the most conclusive: SÄPO had so thoroughly infiltrated their organization that there was no way the operation could have been mounted without every detail being known in advance to the police.

So, while Holmér with his army of regular policemen and the cadres of SÄPO who had been seconded to him pursued the Kurds, SÄPO's own research was proceeding in quite a different direction.

Holmér, in his zeal to track down the more or less organized criminals of the EAP and the PKK, never lost sight of his alternative hypothesis – that the murderer was an individual working on his own. While there were few malcontents with a passionate personal grudge against Palme himself, there were plenty who were up in arms about some injustice, real or imaginary, for which they blamed the Social Democratic Party, the Government, the legal system or society at large. Would not Palme be seen by such citizens as a symbol, the embodiment of the state and everything which was evil and oppressive? Shooting Palme would be a blow against tyranny and a personal revenge by the killer on the harsh system which was his enemy, and on the faceless men who operated the bureaucratic machine and who remorselessly persecuted him.

Painstakingly an army of detectives listened to complaints from individuals from all parts of the country and built up a mountain of paper and computer tape. Much could be discarded as frivolous or simply too far-fetched to be credible; what remained had to be sifted, supporting evidence collected and the ultimate version of facts, fiction and fancy presented to the Brains Trust for evaluation. Naturally, considerable importance was attributed to cases of real or threatened violence, which meant that the record of Linder's Violent Crime Division came in for microscopic scrutiny.

'What about that idiot who set fire to himself?' Holmér demanded.

'Per Axel Arosenius,' Linder replied drily. 'He seemed to think that those Buddhist monks who turned themselves into human torches had found an effective way of protesting against high taxation. He undoubtedly hated Palme like the devil but, having dowsed himself with petrol and turned himself into a burnt offering on the steps of the tax office at Nacka, I don't see that he could have been much of a threat.'

'Of course not,' Holmér answered, 'but what about his friends? Do we have any indications of brothers, cousins or anyone who sounded as if they wanted to avenge this Arosenius? He was an actor, wasn't he, and quite well known, if I remember correctly, so perhaps he had a bit of a following?'

'Not much of one, poor bastard. He'd been in a lot of popular movies, but in a supporting role. I suppose his best-known role was when he played the part of a Russian defector in that Hitchcock film, *Topaz*'.

'He obviously developed a taste for the melodramatic,' Holmér observed.

Linder nodded. 'He'd run into money troubles: that's why he asked the tax authorities to give him some time to sort things out, but they refused. He felt they'd driven him to his death – and so did quite a few other people.'

'Well,' said Holmér eagerly, 'have you been able to come up with a connection between Arosenius and other violent outbreaks?'

'Nothing definite,' replied Linder. 'And maybe it was a mere coincidence, but you must remember the bomb – or rather the bombs.'

He handed a dossier to Holmér, who scanned it quickly.

'Oh, the Tingström saga,' he said. 'What a bloody mess that was. But what about it? This crazy Tingström goes and puts a bomb in the tax office in Stockholm. What's the connection with Arosenius?'

'Remember where the second bomb exploded?'

'At the local tax office at Nacka, where our acting friend played his last part,' mused Holmér.

'That's not all. Another bomb went off a short time afterwards, also in Nacka, this time in the house of the local prosecutor, a man called Sigurd Dencker.'

'And you established for certain that all three bombs were planted by the same man.'

'Well, they were all home-made devices and made in the same manner. They were a bit out of the ordinary, so we were pretty certain they were made by the same fellow.'

'But that doesn't get us any further. You caught the man, and he's in gaol.'

'We caught *a* man,' Linder replied cautiously, 'and he was

convicted. But it's possible he wasn't the villain. The man we put away, Lars Tingström, had previously been convicted for sending a letter-bomb to someone. He was an engineer, you know. Anyway, the prosecutor in this case against him at Nacka was Dencker. Tingström denied all the charges, but what came out was that he did have quite an unexpected motive for bombing Dencker's house.'

Holmér nodded. 'Yes, I remember. Dencker was having an affaire with Tingström's wife, wasn't that it?'

'That's right. A fine state of affairs when, in a respectable suburb of Stockholm, the prosecutor is nipping into bed with the defendant's wife. There was a hell of a hullaballoo in the press. The case went to appeal and then, when the scandal about Dencker and Tingström's wife came out, they demanded a retrial – and nearly got one.'

'The Supreme Court turned down the application.'

'Yes, but only by a vote of three to two. It was a damned close thing.'

'And you think that Tingström might have been wrongly convicted?'

Linder shrugged his shoulders non-committally. 'Stranger things have happened. At the first trial, the court accepted that all three devices were made by the same man. Tingström produced an alibi for one of the bombings: he said he was in Damascus at the time.'

Holmér grinned. 'The court didn't think much of that yarn. He could have come up with something a bit more imaginative.'

'I agree,' said Linder, 'and the way he denounced the iniquity of the tax system during the trial convinced the court that he was the sworn enemy of Palme's Government. But then the appeal court accepted his story and acquitted him of being involved with that particular bomb, but upheld his conviction for planting the other two. But that was inconsistent with all three bombs being the work of one bomber, wasn't it? If they let him off one bombing, the case against him crumbles. Now, Tingström certainly shouted his head off against high and unfair taxation and if he is innocent and wrongly convicted of a couple of terrorist attacks, that would give him two solid grouses against the system with Palme at its head.'

'Certainly two grouses against Dencker.'

'But then we have to admit that he has a cast-iron alibi for the murder of Palme. He was, and still is, in prison serving a life sentence for the other two bomb attacks for which the appeal court, in its wisdom, decided he was responsible,' Linder reminded him.

'But you think that, as with Arosenius, there could be friends or relatives who would be burning to hit back at society?'

'Not exactly. But I believe that is what you think,' countered Linder. 'And here's another idea for you. Suppose we did put away the wrong guy. Then there's a man out there who has already killed a couple of men, one with the bomb in the Stockholm tax office. Wouldn't he be capable of killing Palme?'

'Maybe,' said Holmér, 'but since he is a proficient bomb-maker, why would he use a pistol? But I recall that there was more to the Dencker business.'

'Yes. His daughter got hooked on drugs. She was mixed up with some of the bigshots in the narcotics scene. We had her in court several times, but her father always managed to get her off. There was a bloody great stink about it: it all came out during the Tingström trial. Dencker was away when his villa was bombed, but his daughter was there with a young boy, another addict who had been in gaol. The kid was blown to smithereens, yet, in spite of everything, Dencker went on acting as prosecutor. However, if you ask me, there is no connection with the murder of Palme which we shall ever be able to prove, and I very much doubt if one exists.'

'Then Jacob Sundberg had to stick his oar in,' complained Holmér. 'Now there is a man who hated Palme and the Social Democratic party. And he wrote that pamphlet about the Arosenius suicide.'

'You can't condemn a professor of law at Stockholm University and chairman of the Institute of International and Public Law simply because you object to his extreme right-wing views,' protested Linder.

'He has brought cases against Sweden at the European Commission of Human Rights,' Holmér pointed out.

'Yes, and won them. But you surely aren't suggesting that as grounds for his murdering Palme?'

'No,' Holmér conceded grudgingly, 'but I'm having a dossier prepared on his activities. You never know what sort of people might be swayed by the sort of rubbish a fanatic like Sundberg writes.'

Linder shook his head impatiently. 'Look,' he said, 'if we're going to examine every case where a man might have been wrongly imprisoned or felt that the tax system or the operation of our social services had unfairly penalized him, we'd have half the population on our books. Why, take just one matter: there are 20,000 children taken away from their parents every year and placed in care, because our welfare workers have decided that the parents are unsuitable. Even if they were absolutely correct in every case, which must be unlikely, I would guess that there you have 20,000 potential killers on your reckoning. And you saw what was argued in *Expressen* the other day, that the police don't want to catch the killer of Palme in case it turns out to be someone with a genuine grievance, so that the trial would turn into an indictment of the state and the whole way of running things in Sweden. A lot of dirty washing could come out, and the killer would become the martyr with a great wave of public sympathy behind him.'

'You surely don't go along with that?' challenged Holmér.

'It's not my job to make political judgements,' replied Linder. 'I'm merely warning you of the futility of prying into the affairs of anyone who might have been known to have voiced opposition to some aspect of Swedish political life and the sort of reaction which you are stirring up.'

'The *Expressen* is just a sensationalist rag,' Holmér snapped. 'We have to show how wrong they are. We'll get our man sooner or later, but we cannot afford to slacken the pressure. I want all these damned crackpots investigated, every lead followed up – and make sure the papers know we are in deadly earnest.'

The meeting broke up. Linder went back to supervise his men as they tried to cope with the avalanche of useless information which threatened to bury them.

However, there was no way that Holmér would allow his checking of the records of Swedish malcontents to divert him from his pursuit of what he now termed the main suspect – the Kurds. His original certainty that the killer was to be found among the ranks of the EAP had evaporated in the aftermath of the Gunnarsson affair, but now he was more and more convinced that his man was one of the PKK or someone sympathetic to their cause. So while Sven Beckman had been unearthing the unsavoury history of drugs and prostitution and the involvement of Geijer and Fälldin, and the men from SÄPO were checking on defectors and foreign intelligence bodies, and the Stockholm police continued to follow up every phone call which might reveal yet one more homicidal tax protestor, the main thrust of the investigation was directed against the Kurds. Every day Holmér went over the reports in the hope that some clue to their involvement might have come to light. It was in May that he stumbled on what promised to be the breakthrough for which he had been waiting and praying.

The Brains Trust had listened to yet one more negative report from Linder on the previous day's phone calls and letters from the public. Welander was studying a note which had been handed to him. He stroked his chin pensively and turned to Holmér.

'There's a whisper from one of the prisons which just conceivably could have some bearing on the case. I'm informed that a couple of our non-paying guests carried out a certain business transaction. A gun was bought and sold. What is interesting is that the purchaser was one of your Kurds who is inside doing a stretch.'

'A member of the PKK?' demanded Holmér. Welander nodded. 'Right. That's all we've been waiting for,' Holmér exulted.

Fresh orders were given and yet more men diverted from their allotted tasks. What can only be described as a full-scale offensive was launched against the PKK. The magistrates' courts were deluged by applications for permission to tap phones of possible suspects. As a subsequent official inquiry into the police investigations remarked, for the rest of 1986 the greatest part of police resources were concentrated on the pursuit of the PKK, which had been designated the main lead. The failure of Linder's Violent Crimes Division to get any sort of clue from the phone calls and letters, as well as the fact that the combing of the underworld had also been unable to come up with anything, only strengthened Holmér's certainty that the enemy was the PKK, and he continued to proclaim his belief in strident terms to the media.

As the months passed, there was growing unease about Holmér's obsession, not only among his own police force but also on the part of the new prosecutor, Claes Zeime, who had taken over from Svensson. As senior public prosecutor in Stockholm, most of his cases in recent years had been of appeals against decisions taken by his subordinate prosecutors, of whom there were about a hundred, so he was perhaps regarded more as an administrator than as a jurist. But despite his shunning publicity and his rather colourless personality, he commanded great respect, and Holmér's differences with him, coming after his collision with Svensson, were a matter of grave concern. Finally, on 11 December, a meeting took place between Zeime and Holmér under the chairmanship of the Minister of Justice, with the object of resolving their differences and 'to find some common basis for co-operation'.

Although the participants kept their tempers, there was a definite air of tension.

'Considering the enormous police effort, the results which have been obtained must be considered derisory,' pronounced the prosecutor.

Holmér persisted. 'Bring the Kurds into court, and their guilt will be brought to light.'

'How can I bring them into court when there is no shred of real evidence against them?' Zeime protested.

'Bring them into court, and the evidence will emerge,' retorted Holmér.

'How convinced are you that it is the Kurds who are responsible?' asked the minister.

'I am quite sure. If it had been a private person, our dragnet would have brought in some meaningful information by now. It must be the Kurds.'

'Not so long ago, you went on record as being practically certain that your man was a member of the EAP,' Zeime pointed out.

'Fresh evidence has come in since then,' Holmér replied.

'What evidence? I haven't seen anything,' Zeime asked.

'Come now, gentlemen, we must not get bogged down in petty squabbling over details,' intervened the minister. 'If the head of the police team considers that this is the most promising line of enquiry, it is up to the public prosecutor to give him every support.'

The meeting broke up without anything having been resolved, but in the ensuing weeks more and more pressure was brought to bear on Zeime from Holmér, backed by the Minister of Justice, to bring the matter to the test. At last, in what was to be described as an attempt 'to test the strength of the main lead', a move of debatable legality, thirteen people were detained on 20 January 1987. At the same time, police raided a number of private premises owned or occupied by people with PKK connections. Zeime, with whatever misgivings he might have entertained, had taken up Holmér's challenge. Now it was up to the police chief to vindicate his theory which had become virtually an article of faith, once and for all.

Of the thirteen who had been detained for interrogation, nine were designated witnesses and the other four, suspects. Zeime examined the police submissions and called Holmér.

'I am ordering the release of the thirteen PKK detainees,' he said curtly.

'Good God, man, we only brought them in today!' Holmér exploded. 'How are we supposed to interrogate them if you won't even allow us to hold them?'

'You have no right to pester them further without producing something I can take into court. Your case is so feeble that I don't even have sufficient grounds to write to the court to request a hearing.'

'And is this what you call co-operation?' Holmér complained bitterly.

'I've done everything I can legally; some might say I've gone too far. But we've gone along with your request for the detention of the other three Kurds on the strength of your allegation of suspected complicity in the murder of Cetin Güngör in November 1985. I expect some serious statements of fact from you in their case, and not mere conjectures.'

Holmér hung up angrily. The first indication of progress was the filing of an application with the magistrate's court on 23 January by the Office of Public Prosecutors, of which Zeime was the head, to retain in custody these three men on what was claimed were reasonable grounds of suspicion. This written request came before the court on 27 January, but at the hearing the court threw out the prosecutor's submission in the case of two of these 'suspects' and ordered their immediate release, since the court stated that there were no valid grounds for any suspicion against them.

This news burst like a bombshell. It was a very rare

occurrence for a court to refuse a prosecutor permission to hold a suspect for interrogation. When a prosecutor made such a request, he was far from claiming that the detainee was guilty, and all he needed to show was 'valid suspicion', a very vague and weak term. On receiving this rebuff, Zeime at once withdrew his request in respect of the third man, who was also then released.

This fiasco caused a deepening of the differences between Holmér and Zeime. The police chief's stubbornness, backed by the Minister of Justice out of a perhaps exaggerated sense of loyalty, had resulted in what amounted to a public humiliation of the prosecutor. What rankled with Zeime was that he had argued for months against Holmér's approach and had proceeded only under pressure. Now he stuck in his heels. He refused to continue and was prepared to follow in the footsteps of Svensson unless the case was handed over to someone with a more professional approach.

On 4 February the Ministry of Justice announced that from then onwards the National Police would continue the investigation in co-operation with the Attorney General, acting as public prosecutor. This was an unprecedented step but, by removing Holmér and Zeime simultaneously, the Government attempted to avoid the impression that they were holding Holmér exclusively responsible for the utter waste of all the resources of the police forces for nearly a year. There was considerable disquiet in the country at the extent of Government interference with the operation of the legal system, but something drastic had to be done, since within the police force unrest seethed almost to the point of mutiny.

Behind the form of words of the official statement, however, there was another implication. No individual was immediately appointed to replace Holmér; responsibility for the investigation was vested in the Board of Administration of the National Police. In practice, what that meant was that in future the case would be handled behind the scenes by SÄPO.

A few weeks later, Hans Holmér resigned as head of the Stockholm Police District and went on a much-needed holiday in the sun. While the controversy over his handling of the case raged on long after his departure, Holmér took up an appointment in Vienna, at a significantly higher salary, as head of a United Nations committee charged with the co-ordination of police forces throughout the world in the battle against drugs. His career suggests that there is nothing that succeeds like failure!

6

Green Light for Murder

When Holmér went on leave and, in fact, retired from the case, his successors were faced with a number of problems. There was a spirit of defeat and disorganization within the police, and resentment towards the press for the 'Inspector Clousot' image with which they were often branded. But, above all, there was the need to discover a new lead, an avenue which had not been explored, in order to redeem the farcical episodes with the EAP and with the Kurds. What can best be termed 'the Mad Swede hypothesis' continued to occupy much of their time and resources, so disgruntled tax-payers, right-wing zealots who had condemned Palme's foreign and aid policies, men and women convicted, perhaps wrongly, for having voiced rebellion against the iniquities of Swedish justice, and everyone else with a conceivable or even inconceivable grudge against Palme and the society he stood for, went on being computerized, interviewed and shadowed, their telephones being tapped and their every action investigated.

As a further incentive, the reward for information was increased from half a million to one million kronor. Cynics were provoked to query what was the appropriate price for tempting an informer and whether someone who had resisted the blandishments of half a million kronor would weaken when the bait was doubled. There were some protests against what was described as a public auction for tale-bearing. Whatever the practical or moral considerations, the results were disappointing. There was the normal flood of feckless, malicious and downright dotty calls, but absolutely nothing of the slightest relevance.

Just as during the Holmér regime, many of the police longed to come across some terrorist group from abroad who would cast a fresh light on the seemingly interminable investigation, and some of them urged that an inquiry which had been started into the activities of Croatian nationalists be revived.

A few months after the death of Palme, the former Minister of Justice, Lennart Geijer, had been visited by Bengt Sjönander, a prominent Stockholm lawyer. Geijer smiled when he received Sjönander's visiting-card, printed on red paper. The lawyer was known to wear a red tie and use red visiting-cards when calling on Socialists and to change his colour scheme to blue when dealing with Conservatives. He had won fame by representing political demonstrators as well as notorious criminals, and his petitions for pardons were celebrated – as a lecturer at the Socialhögskolan (School for Social Sciences) at Örebro, he had even got his students to help frame an appeal to the King for clemency for the master-spy Stig Wennerström. Geijer could be sure that Sjönander was up to something. His interest in art and artists was well known, so perhaps it was Sjönander the aesthete, as opposed to the flamboyant lawyer, who was calling. In fact, Geijer should have remembered his well-publicized support for Amnesty International: Sjönander made an unexpected appeal, which he presented with moving eloquence.

'Mr Geijer, you are known throughout the country as a man of enlightened views, a true liberal who is not constrained by spite or petty prejudices, and so I have come to entreat you to give your support to a cause of common humanity. It is time to temper justice with mercy.'

'And you, Mr Sjönander, also have a reputation as a very shrewd laywer who has a taste for the more sensational cases,' smiled Geijer, 'so please tell me what reason you have for coming to flatter an old man, long retired from public life.'

'Miro Baresic,' said the lawyer. 'I am sure you don't need reminding of his trial and conviction.'

'How could I ever forget,' smiled Geijer, 'when it was my fate to have to bargain with those fanatical hijackers, back in 1972? You are not going to tell me after all these years that you have any doubt as to the guilt of Baresic?'

'Of course not. In April 1971 two Croats forced their way into the Yugoslav Embassy and killed the ambassador. Baresic was the leader, and there has never been the slightest question as to their guilt. Indeed, the men made no attempt to escape and openly boasted of what they had done.'

'That's right, and then Baresic was one of the handful of prisoners whose release was demanded by the three hijackers at Malmö the following year,' said Geijer. 'I had to make the decision then whether to give in to their demand to put the prisoners on that plane or see them execute their hostages, one by one. I have often agonized over whether I took the right course in surrendering to their blackmail.'

'Of course you did,' the lawyer replied emphatically. 'After all, where could they go? You knew that, wherever they landed, the hijackers and the released prisoners would be arrested and extradited back to Sweden.'

'Not really. Don't you remember? They flew to Madrid, where the Spaniards gave the pilot almost as hard a time as the hijackers. Franco's men argued that, since we had already liberated the prisoners, we had made an act of clemency, and so we had no grounds to demand them back again. The fact that we had acted under duress was simply ignored. And, as for the hijackers, there were merely a few terms of imprisonment and then they were all packed off to Paraguay. Our request for their extradition was turned down because the Spaniards claimed that what the Croats had committed qualified as a political crime. It took two years to get the extradition proceedings dealt with, and then it turned out to be a complete waste of time.'

'But you did get your own back eventually, at any rate on Baresic, didn't you?' Sjönander rejoined. 'The Americans did accept your extradition demand after he had become a bodyguard to the Paraguayan ambassador and had been spotted by the FBI, so now the poor devil is sweating out a life sentence.'

'He should have stayed snug in Paraguay instead of venturing into a country which observes the rule of law,' remarked Geijer. 'But this is all ancient history. What do you want me to do after all these years?'

'Exactly. Just because it *is* ancient history, I want you to add your weight to an appeal for an act of clemency for Baresic. Don't you think that, after so long a spell of imprisonment, the state has taken its revenge on him to the full? You know that, under our system, a life sentence is almost always commuted, so that even the most hardened criminals get out after twelve or at most sixteen years. How much longer does this man have to waste away in a cell?'

'Oh, come now, be fair!' Geijer protested. 'If his case had

come up for review in the normal course of events, you know as well as I do that he would probably have been out by now. But he did murder the Yugoslav ambassador, and whenever the question of releasing him has arisen, Belgrade has insisted that we should not condone terrorism and that we make the assassin serve out his full term. What is more, since the murder of Palme, there has been a public outcry against all terrorists. Do you honestly think that this is the moment to plead for mercy for a political killer?'

'Why not? We know that Baresic was not involved in the death of Palme, since he was safely locked up in his cell at the time. If you, as the former Minister of Justice who presided over the prosecution and imprisonment of these Croats, were to say that the time had come to set Baresic free, it would have a great impact, and our appeal would have a good chance of success. We must not lose our sense of proportion and fair play because of the witch-hunt for Palme's killer.'

'You are forgetting that Baresic has served only about nine years,' Geijer pointed out.

'And you appear to forget that, in addition to those nine years in Sweden, he spent years in Madrid's Carabanchel prison and was also held in the States while the extradition proceedings ground on. Say that you will consider it.'

'Let me think about it. I'll give you my answer in a day or two.'

Sjönander took his leave well satisfied. He knew that Geijer was a decent man of high principles and a well-cultivated conscience. His confidence was justified. Shortly afterwards, Geijer wrote, supporting the appeal for the release of Baresic. Doubtless partly because of this prestigious and influential backing, it was announced that Baresic's sentence would be commuted and that he would be at liberty by the end of 1987. By that time, he would have served almost fifteen years in one gaol or another.

But not everyone shared Geijer's feeling that the crimes of the Croats had receded into the distant past or that Baresic personally was not in some way connected with the killing of Olof Palme. Holmér had promised the Swedish people that every possible clue would be pursued. The Croats were a group with a grievance and a proved capability of violence; nevertheless, they had not been given as high a priority for investigation as the EAP or the Kurds.

Then, at the end of 1986, a new whisper reached the ears of the police from an informer among the prison population. Money had been pouring in to Baresic from all over the world. Holmér had detailed some of his army of detectives to look into the allegation, which proved to be less dramatic than at first appeared. It was true that Baresic had received from Croat sympathizers as much as 150,000 kronor, but that had been sent to him over the whole of his period in prison, and it amounted to perhaps 1,000 kronor a month. Interest flagged: it was just one more red herring.

After the retirement of Holmér, there was felt to be an urgent need for a new lead. Sixty detectives from the Violent Crimes Division of the Stockholm Police District were brought under the direction of SÄPO, who, from February 1987 onwards, were in control of the investigation. Among the most vehement of Holmér's critics in the Stockholm Police District itself were Detective Inspectors Gunnar Johansson and Bengt Ödmark. Now they were given their chance. Get to the bottom of this Croat business, they were ordered; dig out all the old dirty washing, if that is necessary; go and chase Croat contacts anywhere in the world. If there is a network which reaches into Sweden, expose the terrorists and their friends.

Their first task was simple: to check the records for the acts of violence in Sweden for which Croat nationalists had been proved responsible. Ödmark reported to the members of what became known as 'the Palme Group'.

'There was a sustained outbreak of violent crime during 1971 and 1972,' he said. 'On 1 February 1971 Croat nationalists occupied the Yugoslav consulate in Göteborg [Gothenburg], and in April the group led by Baresic killed the ambassador in the embassy here in Stockholm. In March 1972, another group planted a bomb in the Yugoslav Tourist Bureau in Stockholm, which was burned down. Then, on 9 October, there was a hijack of an SAS domestic flight, and the plane was forced to land at Bulltofta, which was then the airport of Malmö.'

'That was the time when Geijer bought off the hijackers, and they and the prisoners whose release they had forced flew to Madrid, wasn't it?'

'Yes, that's right. There had been about a dozen convicted Croats in our gaols, but a couple preferred to serve out their time and refused to be released.'

'We know all about Baresic, thanks to Sjönander's stunt of pulling in Geijer to lend his name to the appeal for a commutation of his sentence. But what were the next acts of Croat terror?'

'There haven't been any,' admitted Ödmark. 'At least, none which have been detected.'

'There has been nothing since 1972?' asked an incredulous detective. 'Why are we spending our time looking into this group if they've been inactive all this time?'

'Ah, but they have not been inactive,' Johansson interposed. 'Far from it. In 1981 there was a world conference of Croat nationalists held here in Sweden, down in the south, at Lund.'

'You mean to say that a quiet university town in our country acted as host to a world conference of terrorists?'

'No, of course not,' replied Johansson. 'By 1981 they claimed that they were a legitimate political group. They formed something they call the HDP. Don't ask me to pronounce the name, but it means "Movement for the Creation of a Croatian State".'

'I understand that their movement was called "Ustasja",' said Näss, who as head of SÄPO's counter-intelligence arm had more experience of the movement's terrorist past than the others present.

'That was the mob in 1971 and 1972 which carried out those attacks. They were mostly collaborators in the Second World War when Hitler set up that puppet state of Croatia after he dismembered Yugoslavia. They were a brutal lot, and Tito executed as traitors all those he caught. That is why soft Sweden gave asylum to those who got away. But the HDP says that's all over: they are genuine Croatian nationalists who aspire to freedom.'

'And do you believe them?'

'Well, that is what we want to find out. Ödmark and I propose travelling to where HDP officials live openly and interviewing them. Also we suggest going to see what we can find out from the police forces of other countries who have kept an eye on them or on similar groups.'

Some present felt that this was perhaps too free and wide-ranging a brief, but Johansson and Ödmark undertook to restrict themselves to people and activities which might have a bearing on the murder of Palme.

There followed a spell of globe-trotting for the two detectives. They turned up in Tokyo, where they discussed the history of the Japanese Red Army with the Japanese police, who assured them that that group had long passed into oblivion. Their conversations in Bangkok were equally unproductive, although the travel was enjoyable and they were shown every hospitality. They checked with the Spanish authorities in Madrid and had more talks in Wiesbaden. Chasing terrorists is no occupation for stay-at-homes!

Their investigation of HDP personalities took them far afield again. Although the HDP had been formed in Sweden, its president, Stipe Susilovic, was an official with one of the leading banks in Toronto, and the second-in-command, Nikola Stedul, lived in Scotland. In all their interviews, the detectives were told that the HDP eschewed the use of violence in every country outside Yugoslavia itself, to achieve their aim of an independent Croatia. Both Susilovic and Stedul admitted that they had sent money to Miro Baresic for ten years, but they said that their motive was simply sympathy for a fellow patriot and a desire that he should not be forgotten.

'Be reasonable,' argued one Croat who admitted that he subscribed money to the movement. 'What could we possibly have achieved by killing your prime minister? Sure, a lot of us felt that he was a damned sight too friendly with left-wing governments, but Sweden did offer asylum to our people who would have been murdered by Tito if they had been sent back.'

'Yes, but we did put a few of them in gaol,' Johansson pointed out.

'The men who formed Ustasja killed in Sweden. They were prepared to face the consequences. It would hardly have been realistic for them to expect that the Swedish police or your government would have kissed them on the cheek or given them a medal. But, remember, their fight was with Tito. When he died, a lot of the bitterness went out of their struggle.'

'You don't expect us to believe that you Croats are any less opposed to the new generation of Communist leaders in Yugoslavia?' queried Ödmark.

'No, Inspector,' sighed the exile. 'What I do expect you to believe is that the men who fought with Hitler, the men of the Ustasja, are all either dead or decrepit. Think for a moment how old they must be. And we, the younger Croats, why should we be fighting their wars for them, all over again? If we are ever to achieve our goal, it will not be by shooting Western politicians, even the most radical Socialists. What we are doing is trying to keep alive a Croatian consciousness by reminding our youngsters, and the rest of the world, of our culture, the traditions of our people, our national identity. You don't do that sort of thing with a bomb.'

Ödmark shook his head. 'What about Baresic, rotting away in a cell? Wouldn't one of your more hot-headed supporters think that shooting Palme would be a protest against his continued imprisonment?'

'If that were the case, why didn't he announce the fact? Even the craziest fanatic understands that, to make a protest, you have to make the authorities and the people as a whole aware of what you have done, and that it is you who have done it. No Croat claimed credit for killing Palme as a clarion call for the release of Baresic or any other prisoners, so there was no move to release them afterwards. And that was because it was not a Croat who killed him.'

'But there was a move for releasing Baresic, and it has succeeded,' Johansson contradicted.

'Yes, Inspector, a move led by a Swedish lawyer and backed by a former Swedish Minister of Justice, a close associate of Palme. What could such a campaign have gained from the assassination? No, face facts. The move to free Baresic and the murder of Palme simply are not related in any way. There is no connection, and I can tell you categorically that we disapproved of the killing in so far as it affected our cause at all. It could have brought us nothing other than discredit. Go and look somewhere else for your killer. He's probably some disconten-ted Swede.'

Back in Stockholm, the two inspectors framed their reports. Cynical observers commented that, as their expense accounts burgeoned, their criticisms of the excesses of Holmér diminished. As for the Croats, there was not a scrap of evidence to indicate that subsequent to 1972 they had been implicated in any attack on Swedish soil. The new lead, like the old ones, had simply run into the sand. The official inquiry was left with nothing but the weary old search for a crazy Swede who had demonstrated in the most drastic manner possible his sense of grievance. But, as the Croat they had interviewed had argued, if the murder of Palme was an act of protest, why had the unhinged Swede never voiced a protest?

The Palme assassination soon ceased to preoccupy the British newspapers but, while pundits speculated on the prospects of a Reagan-Gorbachev summit or when Mrs Thatcher would call a general election, Ruth, who had returned home, was haunted by the mystery; after all, she had been virtually on the spot and so felt personally involved.

For his part, Sven Beckman very soon regretted the peremptory nature of their separation. It was not as though he was seriously interested in having an affaire with Lena, but as she was able to provide him with a dribble of information which came her way in the office of the public prosecutor of Stockholm, he was keen to maintain their friendship. He saw a way to resolve this dilemma when Lena informed him during the spring that she and her boyfriend, who had been in the background, had decided to become engaged and were planning on taking a holiday in the Algarve in September.

'Why don't we make up a foursome?' suggested Sven. It turned out that he knew Lena's newly acquired fiancé, a man named Bertil Rapp, who was not, as Lena had claimed when she taunted Sven, a cloak-and-dagger agent of SÄPO but worked as an accountant in a privately owned shipyard on the island of Lidingö, just outside Stockholm.

Since Bertil and Lena could not have cared less who accompanied them as long as they were left to themselves, they raised no objection, and Sven braced himself to break the ice with Ruth. He did not think it necessary to inform her that Lena would also be coming along, but he reckoned that, when Ruth saw her in blissful and exclusive communion with Bertil, the clouds would lift and he and Ruth would once more walk together in radiant sunshine; Sven had seen a lot of Hollywood's more romantic productions. So he wrote a placatory letter, telling her how much he had enjoyed their time together and asking her to spend a few weeks with him during the summer. Ruth relented, though not immediately, for she thought he deserved to suffer a little for his inconsiderate behaviour during her last days in Stockholm. Then, after the ritual statements of repentance and reconciliation, she agreed to go to Villamoura. When Sven ran to meet her at Faro airport and hugged her in the approved Hollywood style of lovers reunited, her happiness was complete. The subsequent meeting with Lena was less ecstatic.

'I thought you said she had a blotchy skin,' Ruth reminded Sven.

'So she did, but it's wonderful the transformation which falling in love makes,' he assured her. 'Just look at them.'

He pointed to where Lena and Bertil were lying on a towel on the beach, soaking up sunshine and demonstrating the virtues of togetherness.

'Does she still keep an eye on the Palme file for you, or has she been neglecting you now she's found another way of passing her time?' Ruth asked.

Sven chose to ignore her question. 'A lot has happened since you were in Sweden,' he told her. 'We've had an inquiry working since May on the way the police are handling the case.'

'You mean that the investigators are being investigated?'

Sven laughed. 'Yes, and with all the fuss that's going on now, the investigators of the investigators are in turn being investigated.'

As they strolled down from their villa to join the other couple, Sven explained. 'Although the Government has been backing Holmér's handling of the case to the hilt, there had been so much criticism of the lack of any real results that they decided in May to appoint a Commission of Jurists to make a full report.'

'Who are they?'

'I suppose that the nearest equivalent in Britain would be one of those Royal Commissions which are sometimes set up. This body consists of three men, Olof Bergqvist, who is the president of a Court of Labour Arbitration, the president of a provincial court of appeals, Carl Ivar Skarstedt, and as chairman, the Chief Parliamentary Ombudsman of Justice, a man called Per Erik Nilsson.'

'Sounds most impressive. So what do these wise men have to say?'

'Nothing yet,' answered Sven. 'They anticipate having the first volume of their report ready some time next year.'

'Next year!' echoed Ruth. 'What earthly use will that be?'

'None at all, except as material for future historians,' Sven said with an acid smile. 'But the chairman is rumoured to be having a fine time, trotting all round the world and spending money like water. That is why the commission itself in turn is coming under scrutiny. My guess is that the whole thing will fester into one more scandal but that, as far as solving the crime is concerned, it's a complete waste of time and money.'

'So have you made any startling discoveries of your own?'

Sven recollected the frosty reception of his research into the Persson affair and shook his head.

'Not really, but I have come across what might be called some negative evidence which at least should help to narrow down the field of suspects. Do you remember that, quite early on, the police were able to establish that the shots had been fired by a Smith & Wesson revolver?'

'Yes. By the time I left, they had recovered two bullets, hadn't they?'

'That's right, and although they don't rule out the possibility of a third, they are reasonably sure that there were only two shots, one of which must have grazed Lisbeth Palme before hitting her husband. The police have identified the ammunition, and the spent bullets have been sent to Wiesbaden. I believe they're now with the FBI, who are supposed to be the cat's whiskers on this sort of thing. They have a technique which is almost like fingerprinting the bullets.

'Well, it appears that this type of gun has been in production ever since the days of the Wild West, when the cowboys chased the Indians and when buffaloes actually did roam the range. Palme might have been shot by Wyatt Earp or Wild Bill Hickok if they had happened to have been around at the time. Anyway, there are about 500 of these revolvers registered in Sweden. I gather they're still used by shooting clubs, and all the guns that are held legally have been examined by the police and checked out by their ballistics experts. None of them matches the bullets that killed Palme.'

'What about any that might be held illegally?' Ruth asked.

'Good question. Over the decades, quite a few have disappeared, presumably stolen, but in the comparatively recent past, say twenty years or so, there have been only three of these particular weapons which have gone missing. Any which vanished earlier are of no practical interest since it's almost impossible that they would be in working order.'

'What you are telling me then is that the gun which killed Palme came in from abroad, unless it happened to be one of three guns which cannot be accounted for?'

'And that is extremely unlikely,' said Sven.

'So why was your Holmér running about, chasing those ghastly people in the EAP, when I was in Stockholm?' Ruth demanded.

'That is just the sort of question a lot of people are asking,' said Sven. 'Before I knew about the gun, I suspected Swedes who hated Palme's guts. Now I tend to the view that he must have been killed by the agent of some foreign power.'

Ruth shook her head. 'Since Sweden is such a strict neutral, who would have any motive?'

They had spread a blanket on the sand, beside the recumbent Lena and Bertil, who had heard the end of their conversation. Bertil opened an eye and contemplated Ruth with a quizzical stare.

'Well, that rather depends on how you define neutrality,' he remarked. 'Take the case of the place where I work, Boghammar Marin. We make a very fast, lightweight boat, a tiny job with an aluminum hull. We can sell them as fishing-boats but, I ask you, who needs a fishing-boat that can race practically any conventional warship?'

'Where do you sell them?' asked Ruth.

'Iran,' said Bertil. 'The Iranians stick on guns or missiles or use them to launch rocket-propelled grenades. Sweden claims that it does not sell war material to any country which is at war or is in a region which is unsettled. But what *is* war material? Anything that can be used by fighting forces or to produce weapons? On a strict basis, we ought not to export a screwdriver in case it might be used in a munitions factory. No, our boats are not warships when they leave Sweden: what the Iranians choose to do with them afterwards is their affair.'

'Yes,' Lena put in, 'but in addition there's always the possibility of shipping guns or missiles to some acceptable country which then sells them on to states which would not have qualified for a licence direct from Sweden. Look at the amount of stuff that Bofors sends out to Singapore: that's all resold, isn't it? That's the way Pakistan or Kuwait, for example, gets hold of our latest weapon systems and ammunition.'

'Get back to Bertil's speedboats,' said Sven thoughtfully. 'Are we still selling them to Iran?'

'Yes indeed,' replied Bertil. 'That's our contribution to the fight against unemployment. It wouldn't be in the national interest to take too moral a stand over them, would it?'

'That must infuriate Iraq,' Sven said. 'Both countries are ruled by fanatics and follow their own cults of violence. I just wonder whether this might be a line worth following. I think I'll look up the statistics for exports to both Iran and Iraq when I get back to Sweden.'

'Let's go swimming,' said Lena. 'We're supposed to be on holiday.'

Back in Stockholm, the failure of either the official inquiry or that of SÄPO, in the background, to make any progress had set Birger Trovald as well as a lot of other people thinking. He recollected the hunch of his old friend, Erik Johansson, and their conversation on the day of Palme's funeral. He had another look at those trade statistics, and now there were rumours beginning to percolate through to the media that there had been massive sales of war equipment to Iran from such countries as France, using Sweden as an intermediary and involving Swedish entrepreneurs. Trovald could imagine the fury in Baghdad if just some of the allegations were true. The man from SÄPO decided that the time had come for another chat over a beer and a snack with his old friend in the Ministry of Foreign Trade.

'I don't know why you come to this place,' grumbled Erik Johansson, as he strode into the pizzeria in Kungsholmsgatan. 'The food is abominable.'

'It's reasonably cheap, convenient for both of us and inconspicuous,' grinned Trovald. 'The trouble with you deskbound bureaucrats is that you gorge yourselves. Look at you, you're horribly overweight. So, if you don't like the food, you'll eat less; it's called dieting.'

Johansson patted his plump paunch. 'I'm not fat, just comfortable,' he protested. 'But don't tell me that you dragged me into this gastronomic disaster area in order to have a conference about my physical condition.'

Trovald shook his head. 'I thought that the name, La Dolce Vita, would appeal to a civil servant. Cheer up, Erik. I'll buy you a meal.'

'So that's why you chose this place. Well, Birger, how's business? I suppose you want our help in arranging to sell sun-glasses to the blind or some such brilliant scheme.'

When they met in public, Johansson never gave the slightest indication that he was aware that Trovald's commercial enterprise was no more than a cover, and he never said or did anything that might sound a false note. Trovald was merely an honest import-export agent who occasionally needed some guidance from a functionary in the Department of Foreign Trade. What could be more normal?

'I was wondering if there would be any objection to a shipment of some truck spare parts to Iraq,' said the man from SÄPO, when they were seated at a table.

'You know well enough the games people play over the definition of war material,' replied Johansson.

'Sure, but recently, say over the past few years, as you've pointed out, there does appear to have been a lot less trade with Iraq.'

'Not surprising, is it? Haven't you heard that there's a war going on over there?'

'Doesn't seem to have had much effect on orders from Iran though, does it, according to your own official statistics? So, tell me, what's the feeling in high places about this love affair with Teheran?'

Johansson paused and chose his words carefully. 'Well, if I were a cynic, I'd be tempted to guess that someone in Sweden had come to the conclusion that the Iraqis were not going to win the war after all and that it would make sense to have been a friendly neutral rather than hostile to the country which was going to come out on top.'

'A lot of people took the same view about Swedish neutrality even back in the days of World War II,' Trovald observed. 'But you reckon that a shift of that magnitude must have upset some of the men in Baghdad, don't you?'

Johansson produced the balanced response of the good bureaucrat. 'We had been made aware of the concern which was being voiced not only in Iraq but also here in Sweden. During the last year, there were members of Palme's cabinet who were worried by our appearing to come down decisively on one side or the other of the Gulf War protagonists. So, when Baghdad's feathers were ruffled, the Ministry of Foreign Affairs decided to smooth them down again. That was why our minister was sent out there with an olive branch stuck in his beak.'

'Mats Hellström?'

'That's right, the Minister of Foreign Trade. He had the job of explaining to the Iraqis that the big rise in our trade with Iran did not mean that we loved the men in Baghdad any less, and we would welcome an expansion of our trade with them also.'

'So what happened?'

'What always happens when top diplomats and ministers get together? They tell each other what splendid fellows they are and then they go to a state banquet, or at least to eat in a real restaurant, not some damned pizzeria.'

'No troubles?'

'Well, let's say no awkward problems were raised. Both Hellström and our ambassador, Arne Thorén, went out of their way to keep everything sweet. Not that it's likely to have the slightest effect on the real relations or on trade,' said Johansson gruffly. 'Well, now you've got what you were after, why don't we go on somewhere and have a decent drink?'

When he returned to Stockholm, Sven Beckman followed up his research into Swedish relations with both Iran and Iraq with an obsessive intensity. He had a notion that somewhere in the diplomatic labyrinth he would find the thread which would lead him to the resolution of the mystery of the death of Olof Palme. He scoured the records in the libraries and the archives of the newspapers for information. He bought copies of the annual reports of Amnesty International and familiarized himself with the catalogues of atrocities perpetrated in each country. He found that, while Iran habitually ignored any recommendations from Amnesty International, Iraq usually responded with fulsome protests of the exaggerated nature of the reports, although the records of subsequent years indicated that nothing significant was achieved in eliminating or even reducing the incidence of shockingly barbaric behaviour. It was no surprise, therefore, that a constant trickle of refugees smuggled their way into Sweden and other countries and sought asylum.

At the same time, Birger Trovald was painstakingly burrowing his way through an even greater mountain of material. He had the archives of SÄPO at his disposal, but he also had recourse to some of the same sources as the young journalist. The two men visited the stately halls of the Royal Library within a few days of each other and, having scanned much of the general literature, each was advised that a visit to the Arabic Club might prove profitable.

'They have quite a range of periodicals there, although nearly all of them are in one of the Arabic languages,' a librarian told Sven. 'However, I'm sure you'll find people who will be willing to help you collect the sort of information you're looking for, and help with translations where necessary. There's just one snag. It's a closed club, so you can't simply walk in. But, with your press contacts, I'm sure you can find a member who'll take you.'

'What sort of people are members?' asked Sven.

'Every sort,' answered the librarian with a smile. 'The only thing they have in common is that they hate the government which is in power in their own country. So find yourself any kind of dissident, and there's a fair chance that you will have stumbled on a member of the club.'

Sven discussed his problem with a number of his colleagues, and one of them introduced him to a supporter of the Polisario Front who had previously lived in Morocco and who, having settled in Stockholm, had become a member of the Arabic Club. Together they entered the premises in Ynglingagatan, and Sven was presented to an Iraqi refugee, a young Kurdish girl from the city of Sulaimaniya. She spoke of the execution of students and of the 'disappearance' of 300 children in the city, as well as recounting the routine narrative of imprisonment and torture.

'Do you realize that even publicity insulting the President or the Arab Socialist Ba'ath Party is now punishable by death?' she asked him.

Sven learned a lot about conditions in Iraq, but nothing emerged which appeared to link the regime of Saddam Hussein with the assassination of Olof Palme.

For his part, Birger Trovald found no difficulty in penetrating the Arabic Club, since he knew one of the interpreters who worked for the Directorate of the National Police. Largely in connection with the drive against the international drugs trade, the police habitually tapped telephones, and dozens of linguists were employed to make transcripts of conversations in foreign languages. Naturally these men and women were often recruited from the ranks of refugees who had obtained asylum in Sweden, and some of those from Middle East countries were members of the Arabic Club. It was there that one of the librarians casually mentioned to Trovald that he was the second person to have come with a request for the same magazine articles within a few days. Trovald wondered who this other seeker after truth might be, and it was not long before he discovered the identity of Sven Beckman. Although he did not know it, Sven the seeker had become Sven the sought.

Apparently it was merely due to his clumsiness that Trovald chanced to stumble and spill a glass of beer accidentally over Sven's coat one evening in The Pub at the Central Railway Station. Despite the journalist's objections, the good-natured, bumbling businessman insisted on buying him a drink, joined him at a table and engaged in a rambling conversation. Sven paid little attention to the stream of chatter until Trovald happened to mention that he was an agent in the import-export business and the difficulties he was encountering in dealing with shipments to and from Iraq.

'That's a dreadful country! I'm surprised you bother with it,' Sven uttered with an expression of distaste.

'Oh, I don't know. We don't want to have to take sides in other people's quarrels, do we?' Trovald answered. 'Do you have some particular reason to be so concerned with what might or might not be going on somewhere as remote as Iraq?'

With a touch of professional pride, Sven told him that he worked for the *Svenska Dagbladet* and that he was following up a lead on a sensational crime in which he believed the Iraqis to be implicated. That was really a bit more definite than his research at that time justified, but it seemed to impress his listener.

'Go on, is that so?' breathed the friendly man from Wesyls Handels. 'Here, let me get you another beer. You must tell me all about it. I mean to say, if there's likely to be some trouble, I don't want to be caught with my pants down and shiploads of God-knows-what in the middle of the high seas with one lot of my people not being able to deliver the goods and the others probably not able to pay. I could be put out of business by some crisis like that.'

Sven was flattered by the high regard for his views which the older man showed, and a few good, strong, export beers did tend to loosen his tongue. By the time they parted, Trovald knew all about Sven's still vague idea that the Iraqis were in some way responsible for the murder of Palme. The journalist had been encouraged by the older man's attention but he judged that someone so immersed in the everyday concerns of commerce would never have had the vision to arrive at such a novel hypothesis as his own.

'As a matter of fact,' Sven confided, 'my girlfriend knows a man from SÄPO, our Security Police, you know, and he tells her some things from time to time which she passes on to me.'

'Is that so? But isn't that sort of stuff top secret?' asked Trovald.

Sven smiled knowingly. 'We media people have our sources.'

'Look, let me give you my card. Perhaps, if you come across anything which could affect my business, you might give me a call. I suppose I could always get in touch with you at your paper?'

Trovald, for reasons of his own, had decided to cultivate Beckman and perhaps to scatter a few tasty morsels of information before him to keep him on the scent. The young man might come in useful.

'Sure. Everyone knows me at the *Dagbladet*,' Sven answered with the casual air of a man of the world.

As they left, Sven wondered whether he had not been a trifle indiscreet in mentioning Lena's non-existent acquaintance in SÄPO, but could not see that it could matter. After all, this Trovald was just a chance acquaintance and obviously rather a simple soul, and in a whimsical way Sven felt he was getting a bit of his own back on Lena for the way she had misled him about Bertil. But, as if to rebuke him for claiming Lena as his girlfriend to a perfect stranger, there was a letter from Ruth waiting for him when he got back to his apartment. With a sneaking feeling of disloyalty, he tore open the envelope and read what she had written.

Dearest Sven,

What a heavenly time that was in Portugal! And now that I am back in Britain, I realize how much I miss you. How are you getting on with your sleuthing after the murderer?

I was talking over what you said to me with Daddy and he was very interested. You know that he is a practising psychiatrist, and he sometimes acts as a consultant to the police. Anyway, he thought it very odd that the man who killed Palme was absolutely silent when he made the attack. That is what you told me, isn't it? Daddy says that someone who is obsessed with a sense of wrong which he wants to avenge is virtually certain to make sure that his victim knows what it is all about – he will almost certainly shout some obscenity or cry out that he is taking vengeance, but to say not a word is usually the sign of a trained killer, a professional acting under orders who is not in any way emotionally involved with the victim. Doesn't that rather make nonsense of the police idea that it's some aggrieved Swede who doesn't like paying taxes or something?' Anyway, darling, I hope that is some help to you. And it does fit in with what you said to me, that one would have expected that a killer who was protesting, and taking Palme as a symbol of whatever he detested, would have made some sort of public statement after the event to draw attention to his reason for killing. Apparently, such 'protest killers' rarely attempt to escape but wait to be arrested; it adds point to their action, or so they think.

Sven crammed the letter into his pocket and reflected on what Ruth's father had said. It bore out his own impression that, unless the killer was a deaf mute, and illiterate into the bargain, the chances of his being a man with a grievance to air were minimal. The irresistible conclusion was that, unless the murder was an absolutely wanton and motiveless act, a theory which seemed highly unlikely in the light of the apparent care and forethought shown by the assassin, the reason for the crime was not to register a protest about something which had already occurred but to try to prevent the occurrence of something which might happen. But what could it be that needed to be prevented by so drastic an act?

If Holmér had been misguided in his attempt to pin the responsibility for the assassination on the Kurds, SÄPO had good reasons to keep a watchful eye on some of them, particularly those claiming to be fleeing from Iraqi persecution.

A typical event happened one spring morning in 1985. About a hundred metres from the Amaranten Hotel, a modern, de luxe establishment catering for the wealthy, at No. 37 Kungsholmsgatan is a building whose clientele is habitually much more down-market, the Aliens Division Office of the Stockholm Police District. At nine o'clock, a diminutive figure crept inside and presented himself at the reception desk. His dark features were travel-stained, and his shabby clothes were soiled and threadbare. When the policeman on duty asked him what he wanted, the stranger looked around him anxiously before answering.

'I wish to have political asylum,' he muttered.

The policeman nodded. Just one more poor wretch, he thought, as he handed the man the form, a single sheet printed in four languages, headed 'Application for Permit etc.' The man wrote in English, slowly and hesitantly, handed in the completed form and slunk into a corner, away from other people, and waited. After some twenty minutes, a soberly dressed woman in her fifties told him to follow her and led him into a small interview-room.

'Please sit down,' said the woman with a friendly smile. 'My name is Sigun Ekström, and I am a Chief Detective Inspector. Now, I see from your form that you speak English.' The man nodded nervously. 'What other languages do you speak?'

'Kurdish. I also speak Arabic and some French, but not much.'

'Good. Let's try using English, but if you find it too difficult, say so and I shall send for an Arabic interpreter.'

'That is kind, but I would rather speak only with you and not with some other person present. I have fear, you understand?'

'I quite understand that you are afraid,' replied Sigun Ekström. 'So let's start.'

Although she gave no sign of it, the detective already had some suspicions that the man who cringed before her was not what he seemed. She ran quickly through the form with him. His name was Omar Abdulkader, born on 14 April 1956, and he was an Iraqi citizen.

'That is right,' assented the man.

'You came from Iraq. Why have you come to Sweden?'

'I am seeking political asylum. We Kurds are persecuted.'

'Yes, well, we shall come to that in a minute. Now, have you a passport?'

'No.'

'Why not? Did you destroy it?'

'No, but I threw it away.'

Sigun Ekström stared at him, and Omar Abdulkader shifted nervously in his seat.

'Very well. Now tell me how you managed to get to Sweden.'

The man relaxed, as if he knew that now he was on safer ground. 'It was not easy, and it has taken me two whole weeks. I

THE MINISTER OF JUSTICE
S·103 33 STOCKHOLM, SWEDEN
TELEPHONE: 763 47 28

JUSTITIEKANSLERN
Ink. 1988 -06- 10
Dnr

JUSTITIEDEPARTEMENTET
Registration
Ink. 1988 -06-
Dnr. 88-2024

HEMLIG

1988-06-0

Stockholm May 4 1988

To the relevant British Authority

Mr Ebbe Carlsson is a Swedish book publisher with
a previous career in journalism, politics and central
government. On my behalf he handles certain very
delicate fact-finding missions in connection with
the murder of the late Prime Minister Olof Palme.

On my authority, Mr Carlsson has contacted you
through inofficial channels to try and confirm some
information regarding the background to the murder.
We believe your Service possesses such information.

As mr Carlsson is not only and old personal friend
but also has experience in this field, I can guarantee
that he will handle any information given to him
according to your instructions as regards confidentiality etc.

He will also be able and authorized to answer any
of your questions in this case.

I am grateful for all help you can give to mr
Carlsson.

Anna-Greta Leijon
Minister of Justice

1988-06-01

Ad acta.

Letter from Anna Greta Leijon authorizing Ebbe Carlsson
to approach British security forces

Holger Romander *(right)* Chief of National Police, retired January 1988 and Sven Åke Hjälmroth, Head of SÄPO, now chief of Stockholm Police District

Per Göran Näss, Head of Counter-Espionage, SÄPO, replaced January 1988

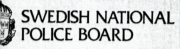

Advertisement in *International
Herald Tribune*, 20 November
1987, offering reward of
50,000,000 Kronor

Hans Holmér, Head of
Stockholm Police District,
resigned February 1987

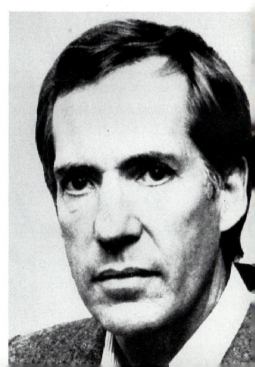

Stig Bergling, alias Eugen
Sandberg, Soviet spy who
escaped to the USSR with the aid
of Finnish intelligence

Svensken som fick livstid i krigets Irak

Av PETER ÖHMAN

Wolfgang Granlund, 38, från Malmö är den svensk som dömts till livstids fängelse för spioneri i Irak.

Utanför fängelset väntar hans 25-åriga hustru Bhagwandai och parets ettåriga dotter på en benådning.

— Den kan dröja länge, säger ambassadör Arne Thorén, som förhandlar med myndigheterna.

— De får träffa Wolfgang med jämna mellanrum och förse honom med böcker, mat och hygienartiklar. Senast de träffade honom var för ett par dagar sedan. Då tycktes han vara i god fysisk form, men djupt deprimerad efter domen, säger Arne Thorén till Expressen.

Ännu vet inte de svenska myndigheterna den exakta anledningen till livstidsdomen, eftersom domstolen vägrar lämna ut handlingarna.

— Vi har förhandlat sedan Granlund greps i januari för att få ta del av dem men har ännu inte hört något. Inte förrän vi har domslutet kan vi arbeta för en benådning, säger Arne Thorén.

Stängda dörrar

Rättegången hölls bakom stängda dörrar i en revolutionsdomstol för två veckor sedan. Domstolen utsåg själv Granlunds försvarsadvokat, och ingen från svenska ambassaden tilläts närvara.

Någon möjlighet att överklaga livstidsdomen finns inte.

— Vid vissa högtidsdagar brukar presidenten benåda fångar. Men det kan dröja flera år innan en sådan ansökan är behandlad, säger Arne Thorén.

En livstidsdom innebär i praktiken 20 års fängelse, som kan förkortas till 15 år vid gott uppförande.

15 år i ett irakiskt fängelse är en mycket lång tid.

— Han får inte säga något om förhållandena i fängelset när vi träffas. Men standarden är långt ifrån den svenska, säger Thorén.

Svartväxling

Granlund anklagas för spioneri och valutabrott. Spioneriet skulle ha bestått i att han i brev till sin arbetsgivare berättat om situationen i krigets Irak. Om

Wolfgang Granlund dömde till livstids fängelse i Irak. Ha har ingen möjlighet att över klaga.

matköer, bombhot och korrup tion. Valutabrottet skulle ha va rit svartväxling i mindre skala.

Wolfgang Granlund komme från Malmö och jobbade vid g pandet sedan två år som filia chef för ett stort tyskt trans portföretag i Bagdad.

Wolfgang Granlund, hostage in Iraqi jail since January 1987

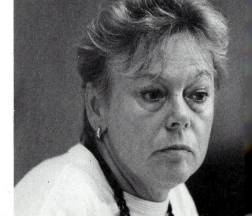

Anna Greta Leijon,
Minister of Justice, resigned
August 1988

was already living in the mountains not far from the border, and I walked into Turkey, travelling at night and keeping to little paths which I knew. Then I used buses. It took me three days, but I got to Istanbul. I had no idea how to go on, but I thought that I would find someone there to help me.'

'And did you?'

'Well, yes. There was a man who sold me a passport, a Moroccan one, because he said that I could pass for someone from that part of the world. He seemed to know his way around.'

'Where did you meet him?'

'In Karaköy – that's a district of Istanbul. We met in a coffee shop, and he arranged for my photograph to be stuck into the passport, and he got me a Bulgarian visa and one for East Germany.'

'Were they real or false?'

The man shrugged his shoulders. 'I wouldn't know, and I didn't ask. He also fixed me up with an air ticket.'

'How much did you pay this man?'

'Two thousand American dollars.'

'I see. Then what happened?'

'I took a train to Sofia, and from there I used the air ticket to Berlin.'

'And how did you get from Berlin to Stockholm?'

'I did what this man who sold me the passport had told me to do. From Berlin, I went on in the train to a place called Sassnitz. There is a train ferry, and while I was on the ferry, I threw my passport into the sea. I hid underneath the train when it left the ferry in Sweden.'

'Can you tell me the name of the man who supplied you with the passport and helped you?'

'He was called Mehmet Ahmed.'

'Was he now?' challenged Sigun Ekström. 'Are you sure?'

'Well, that is what he told me.'

'Tell me, do you have any proof of identity, an identity card or anything at all?'

'No. It would not have been wise for me to carry anything like that.'

'OK. Tell me now why you want asylum.'

'In Iraq, it is not good to be a Kurd. In fact, anyone who is not a member of the Ba'ath Party has a tough time. I was arrested and tortured; I was in gaol for four months. Then they were nice to me and said I should join the party. I was let out and given a few weeks to make up my mind. I didn't want to join, so that is when I decided to escape.'

The detective changed tack. 'What was your job?'

'Engineer.'

'What was the name of your last employer?'

'Sidi Malek. He is an army contractor.'

Sigun Ekström made some notes, then collected her papers and got to her feet. 'Very well. Now, as you have no proof of your identity, you will have to stay with us for a few days. Your statement will be handed by me to the Immigration Board, who will decide whether to grant your application. You are entitled to legal aid, and a public counsel will be allotted to your case.'

Omar Abdulkader jumped up. 'Are you putting me in prison?' he exclaimed.

'Now, don't be alarmed. It will only be for a few days.'

She handed over custody of the refugee to some subordinate officers, went straight to a phone and contacted the SÄPO duty officer. Abdulkader's application was telefaxed to the Immigration Board.

Next day, a telex was received from the Immigration Board ordering Abdulkader's immediate release and requesting that he be interrogated about his political views and motivation. When he was set free, a Social Welfare officer was present who gave him some pocket-money and a voucher for a cheap hotel at Magnus Ladulåsgatan. Sigun Ekström bade him farewell, but she had already marked him down as a suspect.

Two days later, Omar Abdulkader was taking a cup of coffee at The Pub at the Central Railway Station with one of the friendly attachés from the Iraqi Embassy when he was discreetly photographed by a man from SÄPO. The Iraqi told the 'refugee' to go to the Arabic Club and put it around that he was seeking political asylum. That afternoon, Omar Abdulkader was entered in SÄPO's files at their Middle East desk as the sixty-fourth attempted Iraqi infiltration. He would be allowed to stay, but under constant surveillance. That would be safer than sending him back and alerting the Iraqis to the extent to which the Swedes were aware of the routes and contacts they used in getting their people into the country. And, with each intercepted agent, SÄPO got to know a little more about the ways of the men of the Mukhabarat.

Birger Trovald sat in his dingy office, his face a ghastly green under the harsh glare of the cheap neon tube which he was assured helped to give the premises an authentic businesslike atmosphere. In the outer office, a young woman was typing a report which the casual visitor might have thought was an invoice. Trovald was a methodical man. Although his reading of the trade statistics and other literature had strengthened his uneasy feeling that Johansson's suspicion of the Iraqis might be well founded, that did not prevent his going over the evidence against other states with a proclivity towards violent ways of settling their differences. He was systematically working his way through reports of observations of foreign 'missions' in Sweden. In particular, he went carefully into the activities of known agents and those people attached to embassies whose functions appeared to be anything other than diplomatic, men who, in the Russian jargon, formed the 'unepauletted brigade', soldiers in that secret army who would never be allowed to wear their insignia of rank.

He had divided countries into three categories. First, there were those which had received sympathetic treatment from Palme and the Social Democrats and could therefore reasonably be considered friendly. Many of these were Third World regions, poor and in urgent need of the sort of technical assistance which Sweden could offer, and often with leftist governments which found little favour in the West. Angola, Tanzania, Ethiopia, Guinea-Bissau, Kenya, Lesotho, Botswana, Zambia, India, Sri Lanka, Bangladesh and Nicaragua had all received generous aid, while Cuba had benefited from Sweden's open trade policy, buying ships built in Swedish yards. It was hardly likely that one of those administrations would have despatched an assassin to kill the leader of a neutral country who had perhaps done more than any other statesman in the West to help them.

A second group consisted of countries with which Sweden maintained correct if not always very close relations, and groups such as the Palestinians and Israelis, Greeks and Turks with whose conflicts Sweden had not been embroiled for so long a time that they could scarcely be relevant to Trovald's investigation.

There was a third category, authoritarian regimes, usually rightist, which had been offended by Palme's extending asylum to dissidents or by his outspoken condemnation of their oppressive systems, of which Chile was a prominent example. Although there was no immediate dispute with President Pinochet, Trovald judged that, in view of the brooding hatred with which the Chilean dictator regarded the Swedish regime, this was a case which merited special attention. But neither SÄPO nor Military Intelligence could produce anything to indicate unusual activity around the time of the assassination, and the same applied to South Africa.

Both Libya and the more or less autonomous groups of Moslem fundamentalists were something of a special case. Swedish asylum had been resented by Iran under the Shah, but now, with Khomeini in power, the stream of refugees from oppression continued. Yet, here again, there was no obvious issue outstanding which might have provoked the attack, and the same lack of an immediate motive applied to Libya. However, relations with the warring states in the Gulf were so volatile that Trovald judged that it would be worth his while to check up on Iran at the same time as he pursued his research into Iraq.

It was when he was in conversation with an old hand on the Middle East desk at SÄPO that he came across what he saw as the missing piece which turned the puzzle that had confronted him into a coherent picture.

'Forget the Iranians. Not only have they been buying a lot of Swedish goods openly but some of our more enterprising citizens have been helping them to get their hands on war material, stuff which could not be camouflaged as being merely harmless general merchandise.'

'You mean like the high-speed fishing-boats which we sell to Iran and which mysteriously sprout rocket-grenade launchers or are magically turned into minelayers when they arrive in the Gulf?'

'Sure, that's the sort of thing which is covered by regular trade. But I wonder if the French would like to talk to you about the supplies of arms and ammunition, and even an entire munitions factory at Isfahan which they have shipped out, all covered by dummy companies, phoney invoices, trans-shipments or any other dodge.'

'What's that got to do with us?'

The other man laughed drily. 'Just that the whole thing is organized by a resourceful Swedish entrepreneur. I suppose the story will come out eventually. But why should the Iranians want to rock such a nice, comfortable boat and do something as crass as shooting Palme? They would have had everything to lose and nothing to gain. The Ayatollah may be crazy, but his madness is of a peculiarly sane variety. You won't catch him shooting himself in the foot – nor shooting Palme in the head.'

'But don't the same considerations apply to Iraq?' asked Trovald. 'I've been told that, after the visit of our Minister of Foreign Trade, all is now sweetness and light with the men in Baghdad, in spite of the extent to which Iran has been obtaining supplies from Sweden.'

His friend stared at Birger. 'Where were you when Hellström trotted off to Baghdad? Not here in Stockholm I'll be bound.'

'I'd been away for a few months, doing this and that.'

The man from the Middle East desk had more tact than to press Trovald for details of whatever his mission had been.

'So you never got to hear about the great brouhaha over those Iraqis who came here and turned that guy Majed Husain, the one defected from the Mukhabarat, into a human jigsaw puzzle?'

Trovald shook his head. 'Of course, I heard when the case first blew up, but I only got back after it had come to court. Fill me in.'

'It will cost you a beer.'

So Trovald learned that, underlying the surface harmony between Sweden and Iraq, there was a great deal of tension. He was reminded of how laboriously his colleagues in SÄPO had worked to reconstruct the events of the last days of Majed Husain and to pin the responsibility for his murder without any shred of doubt on Husein Abad and Jamila Mustafa El-Chafej, and how their case had been vindicated in court in December 1985, the man being protected by his diplomatic passport but the woman being 'detained in her absence'.

'Hold it! When did the Minister of Foreign Trade go to Baghdad?'

'Mats Hellström? In the middle of February, the 14th to be precise.'

'And two weeks later, Palme was dead,' Trovald observed. 'But how could we send a minister to talk trade with Iraq no more than a couple of months after the warrant for El-Chafej's arrest being issued?'

'That's a good question. Why don't you put it to Hjälmroth or Näss? Mind you, I don't suppose you'd find either of them very approachable. Actually, they were hopping mad. Look, we all know that there's a lot that goes on in Sweden and everywhere else to which governments turn a blind eye. But when those bastards send agents here, literally to commit butchery, wouldn't you think that the time had come for us to take some action? And this prize pair used their embassy to lease the apartment and didn't even bother to try to clean the place up to hide their tracks. They treated all of us, Palme, the Government, the police and our security forces with utter contempt. So how the hell can we be expected to stand for that sort of thing without even a damned whimper?'

'That is what I was asking you,' Trovald pointed out.

'That's what Hjälmroth was asking too. I can tell you that SÄPO made the strongest possible recommendations for Hellström's mission to be cancelled. Some of us wanted a complete break of diplomatic relations, like the British with Libya, after that shooting affray when a woman policeman was killed in London.'

'So what happened?'

'Our recommendations were rejected by the Ministry of Foreign Affairs,' replied the other bitterly. 'This was a matter of policy, we were told, something for statesmen and diplomats, not a subject for interference by mere cops or security men. Of course, we couldn't argue with that, but we then pressed for, at the very least, a formal protest, couched in the strongest language.'

'And what was the Government's response?'

'There was no response. We were ignored and, as you know, the mission went ahead as planned. Eventually, it was from the Iraqis themselves that we learned that no protest of any kind was made. Neither Hellström nor our amiable ambassador had said one single word about the atrocity.'

'What do you mean?'

'I tell you, Birger, the Iraqis were waiting for a protest of some kind. The only question was just how stiff our note would be and whether we would take some positive action which could really hurt them. They were worried and running scared.'

'How can you possibly know that?'

'I'm telling you: they practically said so. The day after Hellström had finished his pleasant chats, the Iraqi Ministry of Foreign Affairs sent a top-priority message to their embassy in Stockholm, expressly to reassure the ambassador and his staff that the Swedes had been good little lambs and had not even bleated. Not a word of protest; not a syllable! The whole matter was studiously ignored. They were cock-a-hoop!'

'But wouldn't they have sent that sort of message in code?'

'Of course they did,' snorted the other. 'It was relayed by coded telex, transmitted over short-wave radio. That is the normal Iraqi practice. We have no difficulty in reading their code: in fact, with our equipment, we probably have the plain-language transcriptions before they do. They guess that we intercept their messages, so they switch frequencies, but we have receivers tuned to all the ones they use. We listen in to all their traffic, and when this message arrived, it caused one hell of a stir.'

'I'll bet it did,' Trovald assented. 'What did our people make of it?'

'Well, all the top brass of SÄPO were back round at the Ministry of Foreign Affairs like greased lightning. "You really must make a protest now," they urged. "What this means is that the Iraqis understand that all is forgiven! We are prepared to look the other way, to condone political assassinations in our country." We had given them the green light for murder.'

'And we were still told not to make waves?'

'Yes, but SÄPO were not prepared to take it lying down. Our fellows kept on pushing, and there was some talk, unofficially of course, of passing the word on to security services of other friendly countries, guys who perhaps owed us a favour, you understand?'

Birger Trovald was silent for a moment, then he said very slowly, 'But we can be damned sure that the Iraqis were aware of the renewed pressure from SÄPO.'

'I would guess so.'

'And if we had succeeded in changing the minds of the ministers, all their fears would have been revived. They would be wondering whether there would be a general boycott, whether their networks would be closed down, maybe whether there would be some disruption of the flow of arms to them, at any rate from Western countries. Isn't that right?'

'Sure. But hold on, Birger. We didn't persuade the Ministry of Foreign Affairs to change its line.'

'No, but the Iraqis didn't know that we would fail. And that was a risk they did not dare to take. Wouldn't you say that here is a motive for committing some fresh atrocity, something so sensational that it would distract SÄPO from its witch-hunt, but to take care this time that their team did not get caught or leave traces? Something like shooting down a prime minister in cold blood?'

The other man stared and thought for a moment. Then he shrugged his shoulders.

'Could be, but see if you can get the powers-that-be to agree with you. They are stuck with this kid-gloves-with-the-Mukhabarat approach. The last thing they want is to pin the responsibility for killing Olof Palme on the Iraqis. You're wasting your time, old fellow. Now, how about that beer you promised me?'

'I didn't promise, but I guess you've earned it.'

7

Kill Olof Palme!

As soon as the facts surrounding the murder of Majed Husain began to emerge, the police drew the attention of the Ministry of Foreign Affairs to the implications of the crime. On 2 April 1985 Holger Romander, head of the Directorate of National Police, sent a confidential memorandum to the ministry.

Information on murder of Iraqi Citizen Majed Husain 510927 –

Husain arrived in Sweden in 1983 and applied for political asylum. He claimed to have been employed by Iraqi Intelligence but that he was now on the run from his former employers.

Husain was murdered in Stockholm on 9 January 1985, after having a few weeks previously been interviewed in *Svenska Dagbladet* about his background.

On 17 March 1985 the remains of Husain were discovered. The corpse had been cut into pieces and parcelled up in two suitcases which were hidden in a wood in Grödinge, south of Stockholm.

Investigations carried out have revealed that Husain was lured into a flat in Domus student block, Körsbärsvägen 1, Stockholm. The murder, as well as the dissection of the corpse, took place in that flat.

The facts so far established in this case do not leave any doubt that the murder was carried out by Iraqi Intelligence, supported by officers of the Iraqi Embassy in Stockholm. Suspected of the crime is a young Arab woman, together with two men* who entered Sweden on diplomatic

---

* I have no data on the second man referred to in this letter. R.F. (See Plate 9 for original document.)

passports. The flat in which the crime was committed was at the time rented by the Embassy of Iraq in Stockholm.

The complete police report concerning the murder of Husain will be sent to the Ministry of Foreign Affairs as soon as it is completed. The Directorate of National Police wish, however, now to draw the Ministry's attention to the fact that the Iraqi diplomatic representation in Stockholm is implicated in the murder of Husain.

Directorate of National Police
Holger Romander

Enclosures: Data concerning the individuals suspected of the murder and a memorandum on the Iraqi Embassy's involvement in the case.

Even before the court announced its decision to arrest, albeit in her absence, the Iraqi agent Jamila Mustafa El-Chafej, SÄPO were pressing for the government to take a strong line over the murder of Majed Husain. In December 1985 their indignation showed clearly in a secret memorandum from the head of the Swedish National Police to the Minister of Foreign Affairs.

6 December 1985   File –*

DIRECTORATE OF NATIONAL POLICE
Chief of Police
Holger Romander

SECRET
In accordance with Section 2:1
of Secrecy Act
9 December 1985
MINISTRY OF FOREIGN AFFAIRS
DISTRIBUTION
Pol III
SSB
KABS
POLCH
UTR MIN

Murder of Iraqi citizen Majed Husain 510927
According to information received by the Directorate of National Police, the Iraqis concerned had anticipated some

---

* The file numbers of all three memorandum quoted have been deleted for reasons of security – my security. R.F.

Swedish reaction to the murder of Husain. In the absence of such reaction, Swedish passivity has been interpreted by the Iraqi authorities as tacit approval on the part of Sweden of Iraqi actions.

From the security aspect, the Directorate of the National Police is obliged to point out that in its view a strong Swedish reaction to the murder of Husain against Iraq is highly desirable.

Furthermore, the Directorate of National Police has observed a not insignificant increase in Iraqi Intelligence activity in Stockholm recently. The Directorate of National Police recommend the expulsion of Salam Noufan Abid and Salah Shatab who at the present time are heading Iraqi Intelligence operations in Stockholm.

The Directorate of National Police
Holger Romander*

Since this confidential document was issued on a Friday and civil servants have serious conscientious scruples against working at weekends, it was not classified as secret until the Monday, when it was distributed to the minister and a handful of top bureaucrats.

Within the diplomatic community of Stockholm, there is a constant round of official and semi-official functions at which news, rumours and downright lies circulate with the tea-cups or the whisky glasses. Information, or disinformation, spreads like ripples on a pond into which a mischievous child has thrown a stone. So it was that during a cocktail party given by the ambassador of a 'non-aligned' African country, the Iraqi second secretary was taken on one side by an old friend who whispered what he had heard from an Egyptian diplomat who had picked up the story at a reception at the Soviet Embassy. How it had emanated from the Swedish Ministry of Foreign Affairs has never been established. It was probably never intended to get to the Iraqis, but it is possible that Arab diplomats who had no love for Iran had thought it a good idea for Baghdad to have some warning of the gathering storm. The Iraqi scuttled back to his own embassy, and within hours Fahdel Barrak was aware of Romander's demand for the withdrawal of the two diplomats.

* See Plate 10 for original document.

Meanwhile, the Swedish Minister of Foreign Affairs had called a meeting of his staff and informally discussed the memorandum with his Government colleagues, who decided against taking any action, but the head of the Mukhabarat was left in suspense until the visit to Baghdad of the Minister of Foreign Trade. Only then was the good news passed to the members of the Revolutionary Council and to the embassy in Stockholm: 'The Swedes have raised no protest; they have accepted the situation.'

It had been a worrying time for Fahdel Barrak. Had he been aware of the identities of those on the distribution list of the memorandum, his disquiet would certainly not been alleviated. 'Pol III' was merely the Political Section No.3 of the ministry, and SSB, the Security Section. KABS was the designation for the vice-minister, POLCH that of the chief of the Political Section, and the last reference that of the minister himself.

It was Fahdel Barrak who authorized the telex to the embassy indicating that the Swedes were prepared to ignore the atrocity which had been committed on their soil, and he hastened to convey the good news to Saddem Hussain in person. But instead of dropping their demands, SÄPO, on intercepting the Iraqi's jubilant telex, stepped up their pressure on the politicians. Unless some firm action were taken immediately, the message would get around that Sweden was soft on terrorism. Stung by the passivity of Hellström, a yet more instant demand for action was sent to the Ministry of Foreign Affairs. It was dated 18 February 1986 and bore the same distribution list as the previous ones. It read:

Murder of Iraqi Citizen Majed Husain 510927.

Referring to previous communications on the above-mentioned matter, the Directorate of National Police wishes to provide some further information.

The Directorate of National Police has learned that the Iraqis concerned with the Iraqi Embassy here have communicated that during the recent visit of the Minister of Foreign Trade, Mats Hellström, to Baghdad, the matter of Majed Husain was not raised in discussion by the Swedish side and that no protest was lodged and that the Iraqis concerned interpret this lack of any Swedish reaction as approval of the Iraqi action in respect of the murder of Husain.

In the light of this information which has been obtained, the Directorate of National Police wishes to emphasize that from the viewpoint of security which the Directorate has to represent, the Iraqi interpretation of the Swedish lack of reaction is unacceptable. Against this background, a strong Swedish reaction against Iraq over the murder of Majed Husain must be given the highest priority.

Directorate of National Police
Holger Romander*

Fahdel Barrak was furious. He regarded the report which had been sent to him, marked 'TOP PRIORITY', and which had informed him of the latest news from Stockholm. He had absolute confidence in the reliability of his source. Far from acquiescing in the passivity of the Ministry of Foreign Affairs, Romander was stepping up the pressure for action against Iraq. Behind him, Barrak saw the hand of SÄPO; they were his true adversaries, Hjälmroth, Näss and their men. They were like bulldogs: having got their teeth into something, they would hang on until finally they dragged down their quarry and destroyed it.

His pride was wounded. Now he would have to go to Saddem Hussein and admit that the confidence of his earlier report was misplaced and face his master's anger, not an ordeal to which he could look forward with any sense of pleasure. Silently he cursed the blatant arrogance with which the butchery of Majed Husain had been committed and which had been taken by the Swedish police as a challenge. If the Swedish Government gave way and acceded to Romander's original request for the removal of the two 'diplomats', the whole of the Iraqi network in Sweden would be vulnerable, and if there were a big scandal, who could tell where it would end? It was likely that the Danes and Norwegians would be sympathetic to their fellow-Scandinavians. Opinion in the West currently favoured Iraq in the Gulf War, but if there were to be a shift towards Iran as a result of the revulsion which was certain to follow the disclosure of the liquidation of Majed Husain, the results could be

---

* See Plate 13 for original document.

catastrophic. The original attack on Iran had not led to the anticipated collapse of the Khomeini regime, and now the Iranians were exploiting their enormous advantage in manpower and taking the war to Iraq, and it was doubtful whether even the use of poison gas would contain their hordes of fanatical Revolutionary Guards. The SÄPO initiative must be stopped whatever the cost, Fahdel Barrak judged, and he had no difficulty in getting Saddem Hussein and the other members of the Revolutionary Council to go along with his decision.

For Barrak had concluded that the only way to divert attention from one atrocity was to commit another, so much more outrageous that all the resources of the Swedish security forces would be fully occupied. But this time there must be no slipshod work by the embassy staff, leaving a clear trail back to Baghdad, and fortunately for him there were at his disposal operatives more discreet and more efficient than Hussain Abad or 'Fatima'.

There was no time to be lost. So far, to the best of his knowledge, the howls of protest from SÄPO had been relayed by Romander only to the Minister of Foreign Affairs, Sten Andersson, but what if the fuss reached Olof Palme himself? He was still the United Nations official mediator in the war, and from the start he had made no secret that he considered Iran to be the victim of Iraqi aggression. Indeed, had not Palme welcomed the overthrow of the Shah and greeted the arrival of the ayatollahs as a first step towards democracy? Maybe he was not so enthusiastic now, but Palme's Sweden was supplying Iran with equipment it needed to wage war. The head of the Mukhabarat did not need to look further for a target. Only the assassination of Palme could be guaranteed to divert the security forces utterly from their dangerous obsession with the Majed Husain affair, and the removal of the UN mediator would be a welcome bonus.

Consulting his records, Fahdel Barrak was aware that Olof Palme took a relaxed view of security; he would often stroll from his home to the office without bothering to seek the protection of his bodyguards. That was good. It meant that the hit could be effected at short range with an easily available hand-gun without having to smuggle in a sophisticated rifle with telescopic sights and then gaining access to a suitable building and waiting for the victim to pass within range, all of which would need time, more time than Barrak judged he had. This should be a far simpler business than, for example, the shooting of John Kennedy. Still, the target had to be shadowed or set up.

This time using secure communications, the head of the Mukhabarat contacted the Iraqi ambassador to Sweden and instructed him to make an appointment to see Palme in person. The ambassador objected that such a meeting was against all protocol. He would be expected to talk to officials of the Ministry of Foreign Affairs and, in the case of important or sensitive matters, the minister himself, but there was no procedure which enabled him to demand an interview with the Prime Minister.

'Use your initiative. Think of something,' snarled Barrak. 'That is why you are an ambassador and not a tenth secretary.'

So, while the Swedish police were pestering the Ministry of Foreign Affairs and while ministers were considering in a leisurely manner whether perhaps some formal protest ought to be lodged 'through the appropriate diplomatic channels', in Baghdad the sense of urgency bordered on panic. The order went out: 'Kill Olof Palme!'

8

Reward – 50 Million Kronor!

Sven Beckman, being a junior reporter, was denied the opportunity to follow up the juicier stories which were destined to hit the headlines. It was a welcome break for him therefore, when he was sent on an assignment to Finland. The story sounded bald enough. A Swedish-registered car had been found, apparently abandoned, in Esbo, a seaside suburb of Helsinki. The car had been rented by a Mrs Eugen Sandberg, who had gone on vacation with her husband – a very protracted vacation as it turned out.

What singled out this story was the identity of the couple. Eugen Sandberg had been born Stig Bergling, the convicted spy who had been handed over by the Israelis when they cut short his attempted flight to the Soviet Union. He had applied to change his name while he was in prison, and the authorities had been most sympathetic. After all, Bergling was a Swedish citizen and entitled to the protection of the law against undue publicity or unfair discrimination when he was released, or so the argument ran.

In Stockholm, the truant couple incurred official displeasure. Since they had clearly changed their permanent address, they were required by law to register their new domicile with the tax authorities. Tucked away in Moscow, they failed to comply, and the more percipient Swedish bureaucrats reluctantly concluded that, having flitted to the USSR, Mr and Mrs Sandberg had no intention of returning to their native land and continuing, like good, law-abiding citizens, to pay their taxes in Sweden.

Meanwhile, Sven, in Helsinki, felt a vague unease with the official version of Bergling/Sandberg's escape. It was stated that the fugitive had driven, or been driven, from Helsinki in another car, possibly a Soviet diplomatic vehicle, and that they had crossed the frontier at or near the official border post at Vaalimaa. What struck Sven, ever hopeful of a story, was that they had abandoned their rented car at a spot on the coast. Why not pick up their getaway car in the centre of Helsinki, where there was always plenty of traffic and where a couple getting into a car at some busy crossroads or outside a hotel would not attract any attention, even if the vehicle was in fact from the Soviet Embassy? Perhaps it meant nothing, yet Sven felt that the story did not quite ring true. However, although he questioned many people, he was unable to find anything definite to substantiate his suspicion.

Months later, when his investigation into the Palme murder had brought him into contact with members of the security forces, Sven learned that his instinct had been right. The story which had been handed out, and which is still the accepted version, was an invention of the Soviet and the Finnish disinformation experts. In fact, Mr and Mrs Sandberg had abandoned their rented car at Esbo, because they had a rendezvous with a small motorboat, belonging to Baltflot, the Russian Baltic Fleet, and their escape had been approved by the Finnish Secret Service. If Sven had only been able to get this information during his assignment, he would have had a real scoop, and even now, if he were to file it and it were to be published, it would cause more than a ripple of interest.

But at the time of its release the official version was sufficiently sensational to arouse excitement and pose the Government some awkward questions. It was ironic that while Sven, who had an inkling of the truth, was sniffing around in Helsinki, the action had shifted back to Stockholm, where the newsmen and women on the spot were having a field-day.

Not unnaturally, the men from the media wanted to know how it was that a man serving a life sentence should have been at liberty and able to proceed undetected, or at any rate unimpeded, out of the country. Someone was to blame, and they howled for blood.

Sten Wickbom, the Minister of Justice, appeared on television and pointed out, reasonably enough, that the prison administration had merely been abiding by the rules which had been laid down by Parliament. Neither he nor any other member of the Government had the right to interfere. Here was the case of a man who had served six or seven years of his sentence and who would in the normal course of events come up for parole within a few years anyway. Prisoners were released for short periods in order that their rehabilitation into society might be more easily effected, or at any rate that was the official philosophy.

That was all very well, argued the interviewer, but surely this was an exceptional case, and the minister ought to have intervened to prevent a known security risk being let out.

That would have been unconstitutional behaviour, stated Wickbom.

The media were not satisfied by this bland acceptance of the unaccountability of the Ministry of Justice. Their annoyance was heightened when it became known that Bergling had been assisted by the prison administration in changing not only his name but also his face, by plastic surgery. This was just another instance of their benevolence towards convicted criminals in order to set them on the road to reintegration into society as reformed characters. As it turned out, Bergling had not reformed, but they could not be expected always to be right, could they? Better luck next time.

The dissatisfaction with Wickbom was not confined to what the press mistakenly considered to be his mishandling of the Bergling affair. This was coupled with the failure to get anywhere in the interminable investigation into the assassination of Palme. Criticism had been mounting for months, and undoubtedly Wickbom felt increasingly oppressed by it. Ultimately, on 19 October, while still strenuously disclaiming responsibility for the escape of Bergling, he took the opportunity it offered to tender his resignation.

Sven Beckman was in a bad mood. There had been a good story, but his banishment to Finland meant that it had passed him by. However, he did get the chance to exchange a bit of background gossip when he ran into Lena a few weeks after his return.

'Well, I think poor old Wickbom got a rough deal,' Lena announced. 'My boss was saying he was a damned good lawyer when he was a judge in one of the appeal courts in the north. And remember the scandal about Rainer, that smooth operator whom Palme first appointed as Minister of Justice when he got back to office in 1982?'

'Vaguely,' Sven answered. 'Didn't he get into some sort of trouble about tax-dodging?'

'Trouble!' exclaimed Lena. 'There was a bloody great row when it was disclosed that he had a secret Swiss bank account. How could the Government go ahead with the campaign it had planned against the "black economy" with Rainer actually signing the notices condemning the very things he was doing? Well, Sten Wickbom was drafted in – that would have been in 1984, and no one could breathe a word of scandal about him. Mind you, he was a bit of a dry old stick, by the sound of things, very correct, you know, always sticking to the rules.'

'Not a bad thing for a Minister of Justice,' Sven remarked wryly.

'No, well, I mean he wasn't like Geijer used to be, full of new ideas and anxious to reform everything. Still, it isn't fair the way you guys on the papers hounded him out of his job.'

'Come on, now, Lena. You don't mean to say that convicted spies should be allowed to roam about wherever they like and then take off when they feel like it! I'm surprised the prison administration didn't give him a new passport while they were about it.'

'You don't need a passport to get into Finland,' Lena reminded him.

'That's right, and I don't suppose the Russians objected because he hadn't applied for a visa,' commented Sven.

'But he didn't do anything wrong – Wickbom I mean,' Lena said indignantly. 'This Bergling, or Sandberg, was going to be due for parole. That has nothing to do with the Minister of Justice: it's a procedure which is laid down and applied to everyone. Maybe the system should be changed, but that's no reason for persecuting Wickbom, who had nothing to do with it.'

'My dear Lena,' laughed Sven. 'You know as well as I do that this Bergling business wasn't the real reason for Wickbom's resignation. If he *is* a victim, it's not of the press but of Hans Holmér. Ask your boss, Svensson, why he resigned as public prosecutor, then ask his boss, Zeime, why he did the same thing nearly a year later. Both of them had clashed with Holmér, and on both occasions it was Wickbom who had backed Holmér. And then to appoint the Attorney General as public prosecutor because there was no one else to do the job – why, I'm not even sure that was strictly legal!'

'I know all about that,' retorted Lena. 'But Wickbom was only carrying out a policy which had been agreed by the whole Government and had the backing of Parliament, so why pick on him?'

'Because, as Minister of Justice, he was the member of that Government who was expected to carry the can. After all, if he had disagreed with their policy, he could have resigned then. No, Sten Wickbom allowed himself to be labelled as the man who backed Holmér, and ever since they got rid of Holmér, Wickbom has been unhappy. We think he was looking for an excuse to resign, and this Bergling business fitted the bill. Otherwise he could have argued, like you, that he was only doing his job over the Palme business and, as he kept on saying, when Bergling defected, it was nothing to do with him. Anyway, changing the subject, what do your chiefs make of the new minister?'

'Anna Greta Leijon? Well, what do you expect? The Public Prosecutor's Office is not famous for its advanced views, so when, for the first time ever, a woman gets the job, I thought some of the real old chauvinists were going to burst a blood vessel. And do you know that she's not even a proper lawyer – I mean, she's had no legal education? Unless you count what she picked up at home; her father was a prison guard.'

'Maybe she had the chance to see the way the law works from the other side, the inside,' Sven grinned. 'She got the job because she's been a loyal and active member of the Social Democratic Party, a stalwart veteran, as someone called her. And she's been a member of the Government for years. As Minister of Labour, she's done a pretty good job, in my opinion, and a bit of fresh thinking in the Ministry of Justice could be welcome. You never know, she might even get things moving in the Palme case, now that Holmér and his champion, Wickbom, have both gone.'

A man who shared that sentiment was Birger Trovald. So many old ideas had been explored and abandoned: hadn't the time come for a new approach, now that there was a new Minister of Justice, a new head of the Stockholm Police District and also a new head of SÄPO?

Back in January 1987, Hans Holmér had badgered Claes Zeime into bringing his current prime suspects, the Kurdish dissidents, into court. So confident were Holmér's professions that he had finally got his hands on the actual criminals this time, that the population of Sweden expectantly awaited the outcome. In Baghdad, however, one man was reasonably certain that the Kurds would be acquitted. Fahdel Barrak considered that, as enemies of Iraq, it would be gratifying if they were to be convicted, but he knew that any evidence against the Kurds had to be circumstantial, since they had not actually been involved. It was Fahdel Barrak who had sent the man who lurked in the shadows and ambushed Olof Palme, and Fahdel Barrak who had arranged his back-up support. Fahdel Barrak was, and still is, the head of the Mukhabarat, but his name and even that of the Mukhabarat itself are closely guarded secrets in Iraq.

Saddem Hussein, President of the 'Arab, Islamic, Independent and Sovereign Republic' and leader of the Revolutionary Council, is touchy about security. Apart from the Mukhabarat, he controls his own personal intelligence organization which provides his bodyguards and is responsible for his personal safety and for checking on the loyalty of all his ministers and senior officers. They also undertake what are termed 'special missions' on behalf of the President. But it is Fahdel Barrak's Mukhabarat which provides Iraq with military espionage and counter-espionage activities, through its Military Division. The Non-Military Division confines itself to 'anti-subversive activities'.

However, since every political party or ideology other than the Ba'ath Party is held to be not merely illegal but subversive, the Non-Military Division spreads its net very wide indeed. It enforces loyalty: loyalty to the Ba'ath Party, loyalty to the state, loyalty to the President. If necessary, loyalty is imposed by terror and assassination, and its 'special duties' take it to any country in the world. One such 'special duty' had entailed the elimination of Majed Husain, but that operation, although successfully completed, had been handled clumsily, and one stupid error had enabled SÄPO to penetrate the screen of secrecy which had protected the Mukhabarat. When the Iraqi Embassy in Stockholm had taken the lease on the apartment in the DOMUS block, they had signed for only one month's tenancy. During that month, the apartment was inviolate, shielded by diplomatic immunity from the prying eyes of SÄPO, but at the end of that period they were able to enter the building and discover the tell-tale traces of the grisly dismemberment of the deceased defector. Had the embassy taken the lease for a year and, at its leisure, arranged for the systematic cleaning-up of the flat, there would have been no opportunity for the Swedish security forces to have got onto the trail of the two Mukhabarat agents.

And so, even after the goodwill mission of Hellström, the persistence of SÄPO continued to pose a threat to Iraq. The assassination of the Prime Minister had provided the necessary diversion, and Fahdel Barrak then followed with interest, perhaps with amusement, the development of Holmér's investigation into that crime. Indeed, there had been no attempt by Holmér to hide his supposed progress from the press. But now, with the impending action against the Kurds, Fahdel Barrak was uneasy. What would happen if, as was virtually certain, the case against the Kurds collapsed? Holmér would be discredited and probably lose his job. An Iraqi in his situation would lose a great deal more. The control of the investigation would almost certainly gravitate to the professionals, the men from SÄPO, and they would be able to press on with their inquiries. Perhaps they would resurrect the Majed Husain case, and if that were to lead them to the killing of Olof Palme, the Iraqi situation would be more desperate than ever.

Something had to be done to safeguard Iraq and the Mukhabarat against this possibility, but what? Another political murder was out of the question: even the most complacent Swede could not be expected to stand for that. If it were not possible to prevent SÄPO's taking their case once more to the Ministry of Foreign Affairs and this time perhaps carrying the Government, the next best thing would be for Iraq to grab some bargaining-counter which could dissuade the Swedish Government from taking any drastic action.

Wolfgang Granlund had lived in Baghdad for several years. He was a respected businessman and represented German and Swedish companies. While he was sometimes driven crazy by the stupidity and unhelpfulness of the Iraqi bureaucrats, he was resigned to that being the misfortune of businessmen the world over, and if the Iraqi officials were worse than most, well, that was why someone like him was necessary, to smooth over problems and help his clients to cope with that brand of red tape which was peculiar to Baghdad. He was aware that the security police would keep a watchful eye on him, that was only to be expected: he was a foreigner, and Iraq was at war. However, as he kept away from anything which might be construed as political activity, and as his job must be judged by the Iraqi officials as beneficial, Wolfgang Granlund felt that he had nothing to fear.

There was one factor which had not entered into his calculations but which mattered to Fahdel Barrak: Wolfgang Granlund was a Swede.

In January 1987 someone knocked on Granlund's door. When he opened it, he found himself face to face with men from the Mukhabarat, who informed him that he was under arrest.

'What's the charge? What am I supposed to have done?' he cried.

'Come with us. You will find out at the right time.'

There followed months of terror. Granlund was confined in the Abu Greib prison. By February the fact of his arrest had become known to the Swedes, and their ambassador, Arne Thorén, applied to see him, but his request was ignored. Eventually, Granlund was formally charged with espionage. Although the ambassador repeated his demand on a number of occasions, it was not until November that he was granted access to the prisoner. By then, the case against Granlund had been tried. The Iraqis produced damning evidence against him, namely letters he had written to his German clients in which he had complained about the difficulties which he encountered in dealing with Iraqi officials and about bureaucrats in general. This was a clear case of espionage, and he was condemned to imprisonment for life as a spy and also for violation of Iraqi currency regulations. The Iraqis have never published the specific charges or the verdict, confining themselves to an announcement of the general reasons for Granlund's incarceration.

When the ambassador and the prisoner's wife were allowed to see him, it was too late for them to register any protest which could be effective, and they could point out to the Swedish Government that, although Granlund was being held in the wing of the prison reserved for foreigners and therefore in conditions rather better than those suffered by Iraqis, his plight was grim.

Immediately after his conviction in September 1987, the Swedish Government issued a statement in which it announced that it had 'heard of the conviction of Granlund with dismay and perplexity'. Fahdel Barrak was unmoved: he had a hostage in the event of the Swedes' becoming troublesome.

The fate of Wolfgang Granlund was one of the many factors which dismayed and perplexed Ingvar Carlsson and the members of his Government. Ever since that day in March 1986 when he had been appointed Prime Minister, the search for the killer of the man who had been his boss and his friend had never been long out of his mind, a constant challenge and a perpetual frustration. There had been changes in the police establishment. Sven Åke Hjälmroth had succeeded Hans Holmér as the Head of the Stockholm Police District, and fresh ideas were beginning to percolate through to the ministers.

Every day, Sweden's ministers meet and talk over lunch. These are not formal gatherings with minutes, but during them matters of moment, such as the Palme case, are discussed openly and frankly. However, there were decisions to be taken on the investigation which did need approval from above, particularly where money was concerned, which were not to be taken over the luncheon table. It was appropriate, therefore, that Holger Romander, as Director General of the National Police Board, should seek out Anna Greta Leijon, the newly appointed Minister of Justice.

'We have to face facts,' said Romander. 'Olof Palme was killed at the end of February 1986. It is now November 1987. The trail has been obscured, the scent lost after all this time.'

'That is much the same as Holmér told me after his case against the Kurds failed,' replied Anna Greta Leijon. 'Even though he was sure he knew who was guilty, there was no way he could accumulate sufficient evidence to procure a conviction.'

'Our own studies of the situation led us to conclusions rather different from those of the Stockholm Police District,' Romander pointed out tactfully.

Anna Greta Leijon recollected how it had fallen to her predecessor personally to express the staunch support of the entire Government for Holmér against the misgivings of prosecutors and police alike.

'That's as maybe,' she replied. 'Are you telling me that you have an alternative theory about the murder?'

'There has never been a shortage of theories, but most of them have now been exploded as serious contenders because of patient research by SÄPO and thanks to the exhaustive investigations which were pursued so conscientiously by Hans Holmér.'

Anna Greta Leijon stared at Romander. Was the police chief stooping to sarcasm?

'I mean what I say,' Romander continued. 'There were serious reservations about some of the methods employed by the Stockholm Police District, but that does not alter the fact that every single possibility had to be explored before it could be excluded. It is only because so many suspects have been shown conclusively not to have been involved that we are now able to arrive at a working plan.'

'I have no idea what your working plan might be, but does it not have to run into the same objection as that raised by Holmér? How can you find the evidence needed to convince a court?'

'We may have an answer to that, now that we have effectively narrowed the field of suspects. Let me remind you that SÄPO have gone through the police and security forces with a tooth-comb, while Holmér has dispensed once and for all with the legions of discontented citizens, together with the wildly eccentric and the downright mad, as well as every recognizable terrorist organization, both the home-grown varieties and the ones based overseas.'

'So what's left?'

'Obviously, it has to be an agent of a foreign power, and our current thinking leads us to suspect Iraq.'

Romander briefly reminded the Minister of Justice of the demand by SÄPO for action against Iraq after the ruling in the court against one of the killers of Majed Husein, and then told her of the decoded telex from Baghdad.

'We consider the murder of Olof Palme to have been a deliberate attempt to deflect us from acts which would have harmed Iraqi interests,' he concluded.

'Very interesting, but wholly circumstantial,' Anna Greta Leijon objected.

'Yes, of course, but we come back again to the amount of time which has elapsed, some might say been wasted, since the crime. That virtually ensures that any case must be based on circumstantial evidence, but, consider, what possible alternative hypothesis remains?'

'My dear Holger, I would not presume to teach you your business and attempt to dream up some other theory. But, I repeat, you cannot expect a court to convict on that sort of evidence.'

'I am not sure we shall ever see the assassin brought to justice. Indeed, it must be obvious that a killer from the Iraqi security forces would remain outside our jurisdiction. We could hardly demand extradition,' Romander observed frostily. 'But that should not prevent our denouncing those who planned and executed the murder.'

'I cannot countenance any further public statements which are only based on some case that would not stand up in court,' Anna Greta Leijon insisted.

'I agree fully,' answered Romander, 'and that is why I am asking you to permit us to go ahead with a plan which might produce the sort of definitive proof all of us, in the Government and the security forces alike, are anxious to see.'

Anna Greta Leijon looked thoughtful. 'You are putting me in a difficult position,' she said quietly. 'I am not prepared to divulge names or to discuss what goes on in meetings of the Government, but I must say that not everyone shares your dedication to this interminable investigation. It is diverting energies which could be employed in other directions.'

'Are you telling me that there are members of our Government who are willing to condone murder?'

'No, of course not, but don't oversimplify the issue. What is being argued is whether, at the end of the day, we shall be any nearer to the truth or whether, with each new allegation, you won't merely spread a contagion of mistrust. And what if you do unmask some crackpot or even someone who had a genuine grievance? Are you sure you won't be making a martyr of such a man?'

'That might conceivably have been the case if Holmér had been able to pin the crime onto a crackpot or a man with a grievance, but you know very well that he couldn't. And, as I have just said, our current efforts are in quite a different direction. I'm sure you're not contending that, if we find an Iraqi, or an agent of any other country for that matter, either the Swedish media or the people as a whole would regard such a thug as a martyr.'

'I take your point, but if you bring a case against some agent, you must take into account the repercussions on our foreign relations.'

'Not at all,' replied Romander, tight-lipped. 'That is something which the Prime Minister and the rest of you politicians must take into account. We of the police are concerned only with finding the truth, regardless of any political consequences.'

'Very well, Holger, you don't need to read me a lesson in morality,' snapped Anna Greta Leijon. 'But, I repeat, unsubstantiated accusations will achieve nothing, and with an innocent Swede languishing in an Iraqi gaol, they could well do actual harm. You must be able to understand why some of my colleagues are in favour of decently burying the case.'

'Rest assured, our plan would not involve accusations based on circumstantial evidence being brought against either an individual or an organization, but it does require Government approval for the possible disbursement of a large sum of money. That would become necessary only in the event of our strategy's being successful and the guilt of the killer, and those who stood behind him, being demonstrated beyond question.'

Anna Greta Leijon looked uncertain. She was wary about giving any sort of *carte blanche* to the police or to SÄPO. The unquestioning support of Holmér in his disputes with Svensson and Zeime had been a traumatic experience.

'Come now, Anna Greta,' Romander cajoled. 'How many years have you been a member of the Government? You know Ingvar Carlsson as well as any of us. Do you honestly believe he'll be happy to go down in future history books as the Prime Minister who turned his back on the quest for the killer of his predecessor, and his friend? If we back down now and settle for a quiet life, what will that say for loyalty, let alone for justice? How will you explain that to Lisbeth Palme, or to every kid in Swedish schools, for that matter? And what sort of signal do you imagine that would send to those barbarians who believe in achieving their ends by terror? And do you really believe that cowardice will afford any effective protection for that poor devil in prison in Iraq who, we must assume, is being held as a hostage?'

'I did not say that I shared the view that the matter should be dropped,' Anna Greta Leijon snapped back angrily, 'but we do have to give proper regard to the opinions of others. Now, suppose we leave the realm of ethics and you tell me exactly what you have in mind. Then, when your proposals have been given proper consideration by my colleagues and myself, I shall give you our decision as to whether you can proceed with the backing of the Government.'

It was one of Lisbeth Palme's sons who pointed out to her the advertisement which appeared in the *International Herald Tribune* on 20 November 1987:

REWARD
50,000,000 SEK.
(approx U.S. $8,200,000 or
S.Fr. 11,305,000)
offered by the Swedish Government
for information leading to the solution
of the murder of
Prime Minister OLOF PALME
in Stockholm, Sweden, on Feb 28, 1986.

The reward can be paid both in Sweden
and abroad in accordance with the
legislation of the country concerned

The informant would be
granted total anonymity.

The advertisement was printed in English, followed immediately by translations into French and Spanish. At the foot of the column, again in all three languages, was the invitation,

please contact in full confidence,
Stockholm Police Headquarters, Palme Group,
PO Box 12256, S-10226, Stockholm,
Sweden (Suède/Suecia)

Above the crest and the title of the Swedish National Police Board, there was printed in bold type telephone, telex and telefax numbers.

Mrs Palme read it again to make sure she had not made a mistake. On a nearby table there lay the official valuation for estate duty of her total worldly wealth and that of her late husband. Olof's share of the net estate came to slightly less than one per cent of the amount offered as a reward. It was incredible. Some little pimp, possibly an accessory or accomplice, who would pass the word could receive a hundred times the entire fortune of the victim, the late Prime Minister. What had happened to the country's sense of values?

But, she reflected, the death of Olof had bitten deep into the social fabric and way of life in Sweden, like some deadly, corrosive acid. Not so very many years ago, an American journalist had reported in amazement how Gustav VI Adolf, the late King of Sweden, would take his dog for a walk in the streets each morning.

'What about your bodyguards?' the journalist had asked.

To which the King had replied, 'Why should I need bodyguards?'

Why, indeed? Despite occasional outbursts of violence and, of course, not free of crime, Sweden was a calm country and its essential character was orderly; it *was* a country where a king walking his dog would be regarded as perfectly natural conduct. All that had changed when the bullets struck Olof. Now no public figure would move without his bodyguards or he would have Höglund or Sandström coming down on him like a ton of bricks. An atmosphere of freedom, decency and common sense had given way to fear and mistrust. Would the old confidence ever return? Lisbeth Palme doubted it: Sweden had lost more than a prime minister: some part of its soul had been killed along with Olof.

And there was something disgusting in the way the sensation-seekers battened on the horror of the leader of a nation being struck down. It was as though men and women had become addicted to a diet of violence, vice and scandal from watching the make-believe world of television and the cinema. Now, when they were confronted by real violence, they grubbed about to try to find a hidden and shameful facet to Olof's life. Like those British journalists who had fabricated a legend of his having had a British mistress, as if that could have had any bearing on his murder, even if there had been a grain of truth in the story. Anyone who had the slightest knowledge of Olof knew that he had a mistress not in Britain but here in Sweden. He had been totally enamoured of his work, which demanded more of his time and energy than any mere woman. No flesh-and-blood mistress would have put up with the scant attention she would have received from Olof. What did the Americans call men like him? 'Workaholics', wasn't it?

And, unlike many American 'workaholics', Olof had not worked like some frenzied demon for personal gain. How many men, she wondered, who had spent so much of their working life at the very heart of the political life of a country would have amassed so little wealth. They did not even own their apartment, and as for the little place in the country, it was far too humble for any ambitious businessman. Even the British journalists would not be able to dream up some yarn of corruption.

Yet it would be wrong to remember Olof as a paragon of duty. He had his faults, but they were not to be found in his private life. He had been ambitious for power, not wealth. And there was a ruthless side to his nature when someone crossed his path or attempted to manoeuvre him into a direction which he did not want to follow, as Karl Persson had discovered. But, despite everything, he had been a man with guts and with principles, as his defiance of the United States at the time of the war in Vietnam had shown. And that indefinable quality, charisma. Of how many Swedes could one say that, mused Lisbeth.

If ever a man was born to be a political leader, that man was Olof. He had gone straight from being president of the leading student political organization into the real thing, and he was only twenty-seven when he was given the daunting task of framing the directives to the commission appointed to draw up the new constitution for Sweden. Lisbeth still felt a glow of pride when she recalled the consummate skill he had shown, combining exquisite tact, so as not to offend the King, with political acumen and the agility of a brilliant legal mind. Democratic Sweden owed much to his virtuosity, and it was a matter of course that, when Tage Erlander retired, Olof, who had already been writing speeches for the veteran Social Democrat Premier, should succeed him as party chairman and as the youngest prime minister in the history of Sweden.

Those had been days of ceaseless activity. Olof had already held ministerial office. It had been back in 1963 that he first became a Minister without Portfolio. Rapid promotion followed: Minister of Transport, then Minister of Ecclesiastic Affairs, a ministry which was reconstructed under his leadership to become the Ministry of Education, with Olof, of course, as the first minister. But all this had been a sort of preparation for the great ordeal, the work on the new constitution in 1974 – that was the watershed of his political life.

And somehow, in the middle of this welter of public life, he had found time to fall in love, get married and bring up three sons. He had been a good husband and father, when he could snatch the time.

It had been a bitter disappointment to him when his party lost the elections in 1976 and, for the first time in his life, he found himself on the opposition benches. Lisbeth had entertained the faint hope that this would mean a bit less pressure on him, more time with the family, more outings to the theatre and opportunities to relax in the country. But, as leader of the Opposition, he was as much preoccupied as when he was Prime Minister. Everyone else seemed to think he would have more leisure also, and they did their best to fill it. He was for ever grappling with international Socialist gatherings or meetings of one peace committee after another, and then came what many people outside Sweden regarded as a climax to his career, his appointment by the United Nations as mediator in the war between Iran and Iraq. If that was what being out of office meant, it was practically a relief when the Social Democrats got back in, in 1982, and Olof was once more the leader of the country.

But when she looked back, the most vivid memory was probably of Olof, head high, marching beside the North Vietnamese ambassador to the Soviet Union, in that sensational protest march against the US intervention in Vietnam. It was so blatant an onslaught on American policies that the United States withdrew its ambassador from Stockholm. And the old hands in his own party were just as horrified: Sweden did not even recognize the government of North Vietnam at that time. That was Olof, the angry young man, the standard-bearer of a new generation of Socialists against the comfortable and the complacent, the middle-aged Social Democrats who fought the class war in their carpet-slippers.

But if Olof had infuriated the conservatives, it was not long before he was drawing fire from the left. Certainly, as Prime

Minister, despite his support for countries of the Third World, he had attempted to adopt a more restrained public image, and that had annoyed the men who were now angrier and younger than him. They resented his coming from a wealthy family – what right had the son of a director of an insurance company to talk to them of social justice? And Lisbeth smiled as she thought how she herself had added a further source of irritation, for she had been Baroness Beck-Friis before she became plain Mrs Palme. Neither of them was exactly what might be termed 'of proletarian stock'.

But if they had known her husband as she did, not one of the army of his critics could have doubted his utter dedication. As she looked around her, she was struck by how few were the visible remains of Olof the man, as opposed to Olof the politician. He was not a person to collect valuable chattels or to cultivate a serious hobby or accumulate objects of some special interest. Their furniture was comfortable but utilitarian. There was a barren impersonality about the things which had been Olof's: that is, apart from the books. There they stood in massed ranks on their shelves, but they too told the same story. Textbooks, tomes of legal and political wisdom, books devoted to current social problems and international relations, the library of a public figure. If only there had been a touch of frivolity, even of vulgarity, how much more human would be this memorial to the warm, living man she had known.

She turned away with a sigh. Everything was depressing, that offer of an obscene amount of money as a reward, the dry statement of the estate with its catalogue of every stick of furniture, and above all the failure of the police to solve the enigma of Olof's murder. It was as though his ghost was crying out, not for revenge, that would not have been Olof's way, but for an end to all the speculation, a resolution of the mystery, so that he could be laid to rest in peace.

And why did she feel somehow guilty? It was the nightmare that haunted her, the recollection of that fleeting second in Sveavägen when she was face to face with the killer, the blur in her mind which could not resolve into a clear outline of his face. Shock had drawn a veil over those features, but the impression persisted that it was someone she had seen. Could he have been hanging around in the street and she had taken no notice of him, but his likeness had been registered in her subconscious mind? If only she could be certain, if only she could remember!

Another person who had studied with amazement the advertisement in the *International Herald Tribune* was Erik Johansson. It was not only the size of the reward which staggered him but the promise of anonymity. Swedish law is based on the citizen's right to know. Anyone is empowered to demand to see, or even to take copies of, all official records. If some informant made a statement which eventually became the basis of evidence in a court, how could the Swedish National Police Board or anyone else guarantee that the identity of the source would not be revealed? Even if documents which are considered vital to national security are removed from a file, the fact that they have been removed and a general description of their nature must be divulged to anyone who asks to examine the file, and the inquisitive citizen can then challenge in the courts the authorities' right to abstract those particular documents. So what possible legal basis could there be for the promise of absolute confidentiality and anonymity? Then Johansson noticed something about the advertisement which prompted him to pick up the phone and call his old friend in the import-export business.

'Hi, Birger, I'm just recovering from a really bloody attack of indigestion, and that reminded me that I owe you a lunch in retaliation for that absolutely foul meal you gave me. How are you fixed?'

'I have to call on some clients. Could we meet somewhere fairly central?'

'You name the place.'

Trovald chuckled. 'Right. See you at L'Escargot at one.'

Johansson swore. 'I guess you couldn't think of anywhere more expensive, could you?'

'You were the one who was complaining about the quality of the food at the last place. Why not give yourself a treat?'

After a ritual grumble about the way public servants were abused and exploited by the business community, Erik Johansson agreed.

When they were comfortably installed in the restaurant and had ordered, Johansson produced a copy of the *International Herald Tribune* and laid it on the table.

'Did you by any chance notice that rather unusual item on page 3?' he asked.

Trovald nodded. 'Someone showed it to me. What about it?'

'I was intrigued by the telephone number.' Johansson pointed to the line in the advertisement and read aloud, "Telephone 46 8 7694109/4110.'

'Why don't we enjoy the delicious lunch which you are paying for? Afterwards, we might take a turn in the park: it should help to settle all that rich food,' smiled Trovald.

When they had finished and Johansson had complained yet again about the stratospheric prices, the two men walked along Bergsgatan and strolled through the small park between the magistrates' court and the police headquarters. Erik Johansson resumed the conversation.

'So this advertisement has been inserted by the Swedish National Police Board, has it?'

'That's what it says.'

'And SÄPO has been handling the actual investigation?' Trovald nodded. 'Strange then that the telephone number is not one of the National Board or SÄPO lines.'

'We reckoned that the lucky guy who claims the reward might be as well informed as you are and be scared of contacting SÄPO directly. He would be happier talking with a branch of the police which would never have attracted the attention of foreign agents. After all, we must assume that SÄPO is constantly being watched and, for all we know, may have been penetrated.'

'Foreign agents,' mused Johansson. 'That explains something else. If Palme was knocked off by a hit-man sent into Sweden specifically to do the job, he will be safely out of the country and we shall never be in a position to bring him into court.'

'So?'

'So, instead of making the reward payable for information which leads to the arrest and conviction of a criminal (I believe that's the usual form of words), it's available to anyone who provides information leading to the solution of the murder. That's as good as saying that you won't be able to prosecute the killer, isn't it?'

'You know, Erik, you're wasted in the Department of Foreign Trade,' said Trovald with an approving grin. 'Now, was there anything else about the advertisement that struck you?'

'Just that it was one hell of a lot of money. Christ, with that sort of bread, a man could retire, buy himself a palace and live like some ancient Roman emperor! Why, it would even be enough to bring a smile to the face of my wife.'

'Better than that. It would be enough for you to leave her and start a new life of your own, wouldn't it?'

Johansson shook his head impatiently. 'Let's quit the day-dreaming. That reward is not intended for me.'

'No,' said his friend, 'but if we lived in a just world, you ought to be entitled to at least a part of it. You see, it's intended to start someone thinking the way we have been talking.'

'What do you mean?'

'Well, consider for a minute the earlier rewards. Now, fifty or 100,000 kronor would be enough to tempt any underworld villain who might have seen something suspicious or who had heard a buzz – that, of course, was Holmér's idea. But it would not be sufficient to set someone up for life, would it? Particularly if it meant going to live in a new country and covering one's tracks against a pack of killers out for vengeance on the informer.'

'I see. Yes, payable in any currency, anywhere you like. I suppose it could be invested at around ten per cent, certainly in Sweden that would be reasonable, so the lucky grass would have to scrape a living on a mere 5 million kronor a year, say half a million pounds or somewhere between eight and nine hundred thousand dollars. I take your point: that is not bait for some petty crook.'

'No, the trap is set for bigger game than a common rat. And, to the best of my knowledge, you were the first person to suggest that the habitat of the wild life we ought to be hunting is Iraq.'

Johansson stared in disbelief, and Trovald slapped him on the back.

'Yes, we've decided that your hypothesis is worth following. Not that our lords and masters are committing themselves to the extent of saying that it's right, but they can't come up with anything better. The more we chased every other possible suspect, the more credible the Iraqi theory appeared, until now I guess it's the only serious contender. But think for a moment, how could we ever get our hands on proof? By the time Holmér had finished thrashing about, it was a bit late to start to search for such clues as fingerprints or footprints in the snow, and the Iraqis were certainly not going to announce to the world that they'd done it, unlike those guys Holmér spent his time hounding.

'No, our best policy would be to try to persuade an Iraqi to squeal, and that would mean reaching someone who's prepared to defect. Clearly, he would have to come over to us, if he wanted to survive.'

'Of course!' Johansson exclaimed. 'Hence the promise of anonymity. I wondered how the police could possibly guarantee that no one would be able to find the informer's name from some official record. You're offering political asylum, a fresh identity. That's what it is all about, isn't it?'

'Right. So we didn't stick some grubby little notice in one of the Stockholm papers but splashed a formal advertisement in a journal which is read all over the world, and we worded the announcement in the most commonly used languages, English, French, Spanish. Our defector will be the sort of person who has access to the *International Herald Tribune*, and you can be sure he'll speak at least one of those languages. It would have been too saucy to have stuck in an Arabic translation, don't you think?'

The two men walked in silence. When they reached Kungsholmsgatan, they turned and retraced their steps.

'Do you think it'll work?' asked Johansson.

'Who knows?' replied Trovald. 'The odds must be against it, but we're prepared for that. As well as the actual killer, there have to be other people in the know. The man who fired the gun could not have been working on his own. Normal Iraqi practice would be to employ a hit-team, perhaps with embassy backing, but that might have been thought too risky on this assignment. But, back in Baghdad, you can bet there are people who can talk, if they wish and if they dare. You don't think that the decision to knock off the prime minister of a country would have been taken by a lone assassin, do you? It must have been agreed at the very highest level.'

'Well, Saddem Hussein is scarcely likely to defect, is he?'

'No, nor Fahdel Barrak, the boss of their very unpleasant security force, the Mukhabarat. But these men have assistants: there are technical experts, probably even confidential secretaries. There are perhaps a dozen people with enough knowledge to make any denunciation stick. Maybe more: secrets tend to seep out to quite a surprising extent, even in the most repressive society. But what we're up against is a combination of two factors, ideological conviction and fear.'

'That's a pretty formidable combination.'

'Sure. That's why the bait had to be so enticing. We know that everyone around Hussein is dedicated member of the Ba'ath Party but, after these years, isn't it possible that one of them at any rate might have felt the first gnawing qualms? The attack on Iran hasn't brought the power and glory that were so confidently expected. Even in the sternest days of Stalin or of Hitler, there were people close to them who had their doubts and might have defected if they'd been offered the incentive and the opportunity. What we're saying to this unknown Iraqi is, "Here is the incentive. You will have to find your own opportunity." '

'Not easy.'

'Of course not. That's why we are not relying exclusively on bringing him over. However, the only defector who would be the slightest use to us would have to be a man of very senior rank, and so he's the sort of guy who will have the best chance of finding or creating the opportunity to get away.'

'But that also means that there can't be many worthwhile targets for your offer, so that will simplify the task of the Iraqi security forces in keeping them under strict surveillance.'

'That's true enough. However, at the very least, it will give those bastards something to worry about and spread suspicion among them. That would not be sufficient to justify the reward, but it certainly is worth the cost of the advertisement.'

Extract from a letter from Sven Beckman to Ruth Freeman.

... and as far as the search for the killer of Olof Palme is concerned, it cannot be claimed that much has been achieved in 1987. Perhaps the new year will bring more success, but I can't pretend that the omens are very favourable. Perhaps you saw the advertisement of that colossal reward in the international press. It seemed to me that this was just the same old nonsense that Holmér had tried. It's like offering every Swede a free lottery ticket. He only has to dream up any possible solution, no matter how far-fetched. All it costs is the price of a phone call or a postage stamp: the cops have the job of checking, and if it is a lucky guess, well, the guy hits a jackpot. Now that they are putting notices in foreign papers as well, I suppose it is an invitation to the whole world to join in our national pastime.

The Stockholm police have set up a special Palme Group, and the man who is supposed to be in charge, a certain Detective Inspector Ulf Karlsson, has spoken to the press. If you happened to have picked up Radio Sweden's transmission in English, you could have heard a commentary. The Radio Sweden interviewer made some pretty acid criticisms of the police and then asked if Karlsson thought they were going to make more progress. It continued rather like this.

Karlsson: I hope so.

Interviewer: But in ten years time, will we still be asking the same questions?

Karlsson: I hope not.

Interviewer: So we can expect some results in, say one or two years?

Karlsson: I hope so.

In answer to another question, this communicative cop stated that they were receiving replies to the advertisement at the rate of about thirty a day, but he refused to say how many of them the police were treating as serious. I've been told that the group is a hand-picked force from all different departments of the police, Violent Crimes, Traffic etc, yet, as I write, they do not even have an office of their own but are scattered over the entire building. However, that is due to change in the new year. It's all very depressing.

Meanwhile all sorts of wild theories are being aired, and the papers will print anything. One kite which is being flown (is that not the phrase?) is that Palme was in some way connected with some arms deals which, if not strictly illegal, were in the eyes of many Swedes improper. There's a lot of talk about shipments to Iran, but the export of heavy trucks by Volvo, for example, has been quite open, since the trucks are not considered to be military equipment, despite the fact that Volvo is the largest supplier to the Iranian army.

Now the chatter is about the huge contract for Bofors to sell an entire weapons system to India. There is no doubt that Palme used his personal influence to help swing the deal for Bofors, and it is argued that India is in a part of the world which is unsettled and that therefore this is a breach of Swedish neutrality. It is also being alleged that mammoth bribes were being paid by Bofors to Indian officials; some people have even mentioned the name of Ranjiv Gandhi himself. Whatever the truth of that aspect of the business, it may be an offence in India, but such payments do not break any Swedish law. So who would have been so infuriated by Palme's machinations as to kill him? The pacifists? Hardly likely, don't you think? And if the Pakistanis were upset by the flow of arms to India, they were perfectly free to come and buy the same themselves: there must be plenty of suppliers eager to oblige.

There have been a couple of other developments since you were last here, although they do not take us any closer to a solution. Do you remember that I told you of the appointment of a Commission of Jurists, headed by Per Erik Nilsson, to look into the police investigation and make recommendations on efficiency and security? Well, the discontent on the work of that commission itself, and the apparent extravagance of Nilsson personally, has reached such a pitch that he has been obliged to resign his post as Chief Parliamentary Ombudsman of Justice and is due to appear in court to answer allegations of misuse of public funds and tax-evasion. There is particular scepticism about his travel expenses, such as for a visit to Cascaís and Estoril. It appears that Mr Nilsson had a holiday in Portugal, then dropped in for a chat with some Portuguese parliamentary people. This made his trip 'official', so he claimed a substantial chunk of the cost of his holiday from the state.

The other thing is the granting of damages to Åke Viktor Gunnarsson from the newspaper which improperly printed his name and photograph at the time Holmér hauled him in for questioning. But, you know, that makes me just a bit proud to be Swedish. I think most people in this country, like me, detest the opinions of this man Gunnarsson, and the whole of the EAP zoo. And, for all I know, he may be guilty of breaking every law in the book, but he certainly did not shoot Olof Palme, so he ought not be convicted of that, or even be charged with it, as a way of society's condemning his ideas or his actions in general. The fact that he was able to claim damages proves that Sweden is still a civilized society. I remember when I was at Cambridge being told by a student of law or history about some Scottish judge, in the far-distant past, who said something to the effect that he did not know whether the man before him was guilty or not but that he would not be any the worse for a good hanging. Well, we seem to have made some progress since those days.

To return to this Gunnarsson. Don't you think it is ironic that a guy who was such a keen member of a pistol club should have been excused doing his military service because he objected on conscientious grounds to bearing arms? It is not only the British you see, who have a sense of humour.

Now, dearest Ruth, to more personal matters ...

9

Brought to Book

Ruth Freeman had been sharing a London flat with three other women for several months. She had written a few articles and submitted them without much success to various magazines: getting started in the literary world, she found, was an ordeal which could be fully appreciated only by fully paid-up masochists. Fortunately, her parents were prepared to indulge her ambition to become a 'creative' writer and were sufficiently well-heeled to support their fledgeling while she made her preliminary flutters into the rarefied atmosphere of Grub Street. But neither her home environment nor the London scene inspired her: on those days when she had what seemed a great idea, it was always her turn to clean the apartment, do the shopping or prepare a meal, and her flat-mates, while easy-going, were bland rather than enlivening company. So it was that, when Sven waxed poetic and wrote, 'Come live with me and be my love', she resolved to try her luck in Stockholm. Mastering the language would be a problem, but she might be fortunate and find herself a niche as a correspondent with one or more English-language journals. Anyway, she was young enough to have a go, she was genuinely fond of Sven (or thought she was) and at least she would gain experience. So she packed her bags and her portable typewriter and set off.

Sven was naturally ecstatic. The ancient Vikings had to endure the hardships of sailing across storm-lashed seas to swoop down on England in order to carry off brides and booty: his woman was arriving by jet, and he would install her in his centrally heated apartment.

It was New Year's Eve. Ruth had been in Stockholm for only a few days, and Sven was taking her round some of his favourite haunts when the couple ran into Birger Trovald. Sven proudly introduced her to the friendly man from Wesyls Handels, who promptly invited them to a beer. He led them across Odengatan into Tennstopet.

'One of my pet pubs,' Trovald told them.

Ruth looked around her at the bare wooden tables at which groups of men and women were drinking and eating snacks. Beyond was a more formal space, where tables decorously covered with white tablecloths were set for more serious dining.

'So you are a writer,' Trovald said. 'And with your boyfriend a celebrated reporter with one of our most important newspapers, you should never be short of material for a story.'

'I'm too busy getting used to Stockholm again to have got down to serious work,' Ruth admitted. 'I was here only for a few days, nearly two years ago. And, to tell you the truth, I'm not even clear yet exactly what kind of book I would like to write or what sort of subject I ought to work on.'

'I expect that, when the right thing turns up, you will know,' smiled Trovald. 'Isn't that what inspiration is all about?'

'Maybe. I just hope I don't have to wait too long. Meanwhile, I'm working on improving my cooking. Don't you think Sven is looking well fed and radiantly healthy?'

'Yes, but I thought that might have been due to something other than the improvement in his diet,' smiled Trovald. 'However, I must be getting along: I have to meet someone. Let me wish you a happy and successful New Year, and you also, Sven Beckman. You are certainly getting off to a good start.'

'He's rather nice,' commented Ruth to Sven after Trovald had left them. 'Sort of cuddly. Is he someone important?'

'No, not at all,' Sven replied with a superior smile. 'He handles shipments of goods to all sorts of countries. That's his job, very dull when you get down to it, a matter of office routine, you know. Mind you, I have been able to give him a bit of help from time to time with snippets of information which might affect his business. I expect you'll see him around, but don't tell him he's cuddly; he would probably die of embarrassment.'

'I wonder,' mused Ruth. 'There was something about him that gave me the feeling that he's not quite the hearty, straightforward fellow he appears.'

'That's a writer's imagination getting to work,' laughed Sven.

Trovald had been on his way to meet his wife: even security

police have time off, and his thoughts were more of the New Year celebrations than of the doings of spies or terrorists. He smiled to himself as he recalled Sven's boyish enthusiasm, positively wagging his tail in delight, as he displayed Ruth for Birger's approbation. She seemed a shrewd kid; having her around might sharpen the celebrated reporter up a bit, Trovald judged.

'Birger Trovald, what the hell is the matter with you? Mooning about like a curate in a brothel!'

He looked up to see Erik Johansson, beaming at him.

'Sorry. I never noticed you: I had something on my mind.'

'Serious?'

'No, not at all,' Trovald answered. 'Quite the reverse, rather amusing.'

'That's a relief,' said Johansson. 'Well, a Happy New Year to you. You looked so very solemn. Come and have a drink?'

Trovald shook his head and explained that he had only just emerged from a bar and that his wife would be waiting for him.

'Do you mind if I walk along with you?' Johansson demanded. 'I also have had something on my mind about which I would like your opinion.'

'Go ahead,' Trovald invited, as the other fell into step beside him.

'First, tell me, have you fellows had any joy from the advertisement in the *International Herald Tribune* yet?' asked Johansson.

Trovald glanced at his companion. 'You know, in my job, we don't answer questions, we ask them,' he replied.

Johansson had received this response on previous occasions and knew it to be a signal to back off.

'The only reason I had for mentioning it was that I've been thinking about what you told me last time we met. It struck me that you people were not being very fair.'

'Fair to whom?' asked Trovald, frowning.

'To people in general, to the Swedish people if you like,' replied Johansson. His smile of welcome had faded, and his expression was serious. 'Just consider for a moment. That advertisement was on your own admission a coded message which your enemies would understand: that is essentially what you said. It told them that you knew who they are and what they have done.'

'I never said anything as definite as that,' Trovald objected. 'I only went as far as to say that we have accepted a hypothesis, which, let me remind you, was originally put forward by yourself, as being the most probable reconstruction of what actually led to the death of Olof Palme.'

'And also that there was no sensible alternative hypothesis,' Johansson added.

'That too. So what is your point?' asked Trovald, as they walked briskly along the practically deserted street.

'Simply this: that there is too much damned secrecy about, and it's not healthy. Of course, I understand that there are times when it would be stupid to blab vital secrets or even to make comments which could be damaging, but that doesn't apply here, does it? Here you have a case where you and your opponents both understand fully what the score is. Why should the poor, damned public be the only ones to be kept in the dark? Why do you have to be so bashful? Are you frightened of hurting the feelings of the Iraqis?'

Trovald had never seen Johansson so nettled: his chin jutted forward in an uncharacteristically aggressive pose, and there was a gleam in his eye which warned that he was in no mood to be trifled with.

'It's not my decision when information should be allowed to get out,' Trovald replied in a conciliatory tone. 'The games we play are not always as simple as they might appear, and we don't play according to the rules, because there are no rules.'

'Don't dodge behind that smoke-screen of "We know what's good for you"! Once we let policemen decide what can and what cannot be disclosed "in the public interest", it's only a matter of time before politicians use that excuse to hush up their mistakes, bury evidence of corruption or just suppress facts which they consider might lose them votes. What sort of a democracy do you call that? How about a little *glasnost*, my friend, or is Sweden going the same way as Britain, where they serve out injunctions in the supermarkets?'

'Don't get carried away, old friend,' Trovald answered quietly. 'We still believe in the right to know, and if I thought we'd become simply an agency for cover-ups, I would have chucked up the job long ago.'

'Great. In that case, why don't you come out with a statement which tells the Swedish people at any rate as much as you've already let the Iraqis know? Even if you're unable to produce the killer in court, why shouldn't his masters be branded so that men and women here, and in every other decent country, should know them for what they are?'

Trovald paused before replying and weighed his words carefully. 'I am not denying that there's a lot of truth in what you say, but you must have a little patience. There is a right way and a hell of a lot of wrong ways of going about even as apparently uncomplicated a matter as releasing information.' Johansson made as if to interrupt, but Trovald shook his head and pressed on resolutely. 'I know you're not satisfied, but that is as much of an answer as I'm prepared to give you at this time.

'Now, I'm sure I can rely on you not to try to take matters into your own hands. If you were to be so foolish as, for example, to leak anything to the press, there would immediately be an official denial, and you would not be in a position to produce any concrete evidence. Your revelations would be dismissed as just one more of the outpourings of the lunatics who come up with one crazy theory after another about who killed Palme. As for me, I would swear that I had no idea what you were talking about.

'Go home and cool down. Relax. After all, this is a holiday, and nothing would be changed if some sort of statement were to be made next week, or even next month, instead of this evening. Be a good fellow and trust us a bit longer, and do remember that things might be happening of which you are unaware but which can have an important bearing on the way we handle this phase of our hunt, and on its ultimate success.'

'That's going back to the "We know best" ploy,' complained Johansson.

'True enough,' assented Trovald. 'And sometimes, not always, I grant you, but sometimes, we do. Now, old friend, I wish you a belated Happy New Year; may it bring you much joy – and peace of mind. But I must hurry or I shall get the sack for dereliction of duty.'

'What? Your boss is chasing you, on a holiday?' interjected Johansson, with a wide grin.

'My wife, you fool! You should know that, for a married man, there are no such things as holidays.'

Trovald scurried away. First Sven Beckman and his girl, now Erik Johansson: that was quite enough socializing for one day.

Despite his jocular farewell, he knew that Johansson was still in deadly earnest on the need to dispel unnecessary secrecy. But Trovald felt that, even if he had been unable to convince him that SÄPO was a totally benign institution, he could rely on his discretion. But for how much longer? That was another matter. Something ought to be done.

Birger Trovald made a formal report to his superiors and also put forward some personal suggestions. Both were acknowledged. He waited, but nothing further was said. Trovald was sufficiently experienced to know that, if there were any objections to the course of action he proposed, he would have been informed very quickly and in unambiguous language. Silence was tantamount to approval – that is, unless his scheme misfired.

Ten days later, as Sven Beckman walked into the offices of the *Svenska Dagbladet*, one of his fellow reporters told him that there had been a phone call for him.

'Some old soak called Trovald. He said you have his number, and he wants you to ring him back.'

Sven nodded. 'He's one of my confidential sources,' he said. He attempted to sound both conspiratorial and self-important.

'Don't give us that load of bullshit,' grinned his colleague. 'He's just some boozer you go around with. What is he, a pimp?'

Sven ignored him and went to a phone. He got through without difficulty to Wesyls Handels, and Birger Trovald answered immediately.

'Something very strange has turned up,' The import-export agent sounded worried. 'I'd rather like to see you. It's not anything that I want to talk about on the phone. Could you come by here?'

'When?'

'The sooner the better. Tell me when you can get here, and I'll stay in the office.'

'Right. I'm on my way,' Sven told him and hung up. He turned to his irreverent colleague. 'I have to go out. This could be a big story.'

'Balls! The pair of you are off to call on some grubby old floozey,' retorted the unimpressed reporter.

Sven beat an undignified retreat.

In the offices of Wesyls Handels, he found a scene of hectic activity. A couple of harassed assistants, their jackets slung over the backs of their swivel chairs, were barking instructions and arguing vociferously down their phones, while other phones shrilled or buzzed incessantly until they were picked up by a pale-faced girl who seemed to be receptionist-secretary-switchboard-operator-cashier-and-coffee-maker. At the back of the room, a telex machine clacked contentedly to itself, and beside it a news agency teleprinter spewed out reams of paper which apparently interested no one. The young reporter was not left in any doubt that this was a genuine outpost of the world of commerce. The overworked young woman took his name and muttered a message into an intercom.

'Mr Trovald will see you in a minute,' she told him. 'Please, take a seat.'

Sven sat down on a plastic chair which pretended to be leather and might have been designed to provide the maximum discomfort. He picked up a trade journal and flicked through the pages while he waited. Around him, the staff of Wesyls Handels went about their business. After some five minutes, he was ushered into the inner office.

While Sven had been waiting outside, Birger Trovald had looked again at the file before him. However, the papers on which he concentrated were not concerned with either exports or imports but were a summary of Sven's record, compiled when he did his military service. They indicated that he was reliable and stable, not given to freakish behaviour, and his loyalty had never been questioned. Yes, he'll do nicely, thought Trovald.

'Sorry you had to wait,' Trovald said, waving him to a slightly better-quality armchair, 'but I had an important call from a trading house in Singapore, and I could not put them off.'

'Wouldn't it be an odd hour of the day for people to be working in an office in Singapore?' asked Sven.

Trovald laughed. 'If the business is really urgent, they'll be on the job at any hour of the day or night, calling from their homes if necessary. Want a coffee?'

Without waiting for an answer, he spoke into the intercom and ordered a couple of cups of coffee. Only when they had been brought in and the door had closed behind the office factotum did he draw up his chair close to where Sven was sitting, as if he were nervous that they might be overheard, and started to talk about a subject more serious than the weather.

'I realize that your time is valuable, and I wouldn't have disturbed you, but something has turned up which has got me very worried. Frankly, I don't know how to cope, but I thought of you at once. With your experience and your contacts, maybe you can help me.'

Trovald rolled his eyes appealingly, and Sven, feeling very much the master of the situation whatever it might be, assured him that he would do whatever he could to solve the problem which was obviously beyond the powers of a mere plodding office-worker.

'Do you remember that, when we first met, I told you I was engaged in some business with Iraq?' Sven nodded. 'Well, the man with whom I was most involved – I've got his name on a card somewhere, Abdul something or other ...' Trovald riffled ineffectually through some papers on his desk, then abandoned his quest with a shrug of his shoulders. 'Doesn't matter, it'll turn up sooner or later. Anyway, this Abdul has apparently been involved in a great deal more than importing paper-making machinery, which was what we were doing together. It seems that he was, perhaps still is, a member of their secret police, a mob they call Mukhabarat.'

'He told you that?' asked Sven incredulously.

'He had to tell someone,' Trovald said apologetically. 'You see, he's done a bunk. He spun the authorities some yarn about having to go and inspect this machinery, in order to keep up his cover story of being an innocent importer, and he got a visa to fly out here. Now he wants political asylum.'

'Yes, I understand. But why come to you? Wouldn't the proper thing be to report to the police?'

Trovald crouched even closer to Sven. 'There's a bit more to it than that.' He dropped his voice, and Sven had to strain to hear his words. 'You see, he trusts me because of the way we've worked together. As for going through the routine of the Immigration Department, he told me a horrible story about another defector from the Mukhabarat, two or three years ago, some fellow called Majed Husain, if I remember right. Our immigration people are so worried about spies pretending to be refugees, and they have so many applications, genuine or otherwise, that things can take a hell of a long time before a man is granted asylum. Anyway, before this Majed Husain had got through the works, the Iraqis sent a hit-team after him and bumped him off. Well, you can understand that Abdul is worried and wants to lie very low until he can be sure of being safe.'

'So why don't you tell this to the Immigration Board or, better still, talk to SÄPO?'

'It's because of the story Abdul told me. These Mukhabarat are violent people. I remember that you warned me against getting mixed up in business with Iraq, and I wish I'd taken your advice. However, it's too late to think like that now. Abdul was very close to the boss of the Mukhabarat, a man called Fahdel Barrak, and he's done several jobs he doesn't want to talk about.

'But one assignment of which he will give details was when he was part of a back-up team providing assistance to the man who shot Olof Palme.'

'What? Are you sure of what you're telling me?' Sven felt a thrill: he had always suspected that Iraq was somehow mixed up in the murder but had never been able to get his hands on anything definite.

Trovald looked unhappy as only a man who is frightened out of his wits can. 'He has a lot of evidence, and he wants to bring the whole thing out into the open.'

'Wait a minute,' Sven interrupted. 'If he has that sort of information – why, you must have seen the advertisement the police put into the *International Herald Tribune*. He can claim this enormous reward, be given a new identity, asylum, the works!'

'Yes, yes, of course, but he wants to be certain that he stays alive long enough to enjoy it. Can't you understand that he's scared stiff. And that's where you can be a help.'

'Me? How?' asked Sven, baffled.

'Well, don't you see that, if his story were to be printed and given a lot of publicity, it would be too late for the Mukhabarat to hush the thing up. Of course, he would still be a hunted man, but the real pressure is to kill him before he can talk. If he waits until he's got in touch with the police and they've gone through the rigmarole of checking his story – they must get plenty of hopeful informers each day, he'll probably end up like Majed Husain. And another thing. Once his story is public knowledge, it will almost certainly be denied by the Iraqis. Now, if they were to knock him off afterwards, it would be virtually an admission of guilt. So the safest thing for him is to tell his story and get it printed. Will you help?'

Sven gazed in astonishment at Trovald. How could such an insignificant little man come in contact with a story that was a newsman's dream!

'Can I meet this Abdul?' he asked.

Trovald shook his head. 'He's too nervous to talk to anyone other than me now. Of course, when the story is out, things will be different. But I can get you answers to any questions you want to put to him, and meanwhile I have the really vital information for you.'

'You really think that, if the *Svenska Dagbladet* were to print this, your Abdul would be in the clear?'

'Well, no, that was not exactly what I had in mind.' Trovald shifted uncomfortably in his chair. 'You see, the Swedish papers have been full of Palme stories, and the truth is that just one more would not cut much ice, would it? Now, if what Abdul has to say could come from abroad, say from Britain, for example, the Swedish papers would pick it up, of course, but it would be taken far more seriously. Don't you agree?'

Sven saw the prospect of the scoop of a lifetime melting away, but before he could raise any objections, Trovald continued.

'There are reasons connected with the fate of his family back in Iraq which make it absolutely vital that nothing appears in print for just a few weeks more.'

'But surely every day that we delay Abdul's own life is in danger?'

Trovald nodded gravely. 'But he is the one who must make the decision on timing, since he's the only person who knows the situation in Iraq. However, you can rest assured that neither he nor I will talk to anyone else, so you won't be cut out by one of your competitors. But what I wondered was, couldn't your sweet little British girlfriend do something with this story? You told me she's a writer.'

'I'll talk it over with her,' Sven replied. 'Then perhaps we ought to meet again and work out a definite plan.'

He got up to go, and Trovald opened the door for him.

'I'm so glad I spoke to you,' said the import-export agent. 'I knew you were the right man to approach.'

At the door, Sven turned. 'Wait a minute,' he said. 'Maybe you don't remember, but there was a Swedish businessman who was put in gaol by the Iraqis, not so long ago. Perhaps, if this story of your refugee were to be published, that would make things bad for him?'

Trovald was on the point of assuring Sven that this had been taken into account, but he recalled that a simple commercial agent would hardly be likely to know such inner secrets. He scratched his nose thoughtfully.

'Well, I don't know,' he said slowly. 'Maybe you're right and we ought not bring Abdul's story out into the open. But that would be a pity.' Then, as if struck by a sudden flash of inspiration, he continued: 'I tell you what, young fellow. There's a man I know who can almost certainly tell you the score. He works in the Ministry of Foreign Affairs, in the Department of Foreign Trade, and he's often looked up things for me. I know he's done a lot of homework on Iraq. Here, I'll give you his name and the extension where you can contact him. Tell him I told you to get in touch with him.'

He scribbled on a piece of paper which he handed to Sven.

'Erik Johansson,' Sven read. 'OK. I'll call him right away, and I'll let you know how I get on.'

After Sven had left, Birger smiled to himself. The arrival of the eager cub reporter should convince his old friend that he was in earnest in his promise that the Swedish people would be told the truth – or, at least, that part of it that was good for them – eventually. Then he put through a call.

'I think it will work,' he reported. 'And we can be sure that nothing will come out until at least a couple of months after the appearance of our advertisement, by which time anyone who ought to be interested will have had plenty of time and it will have served its purpose.'

Erik Johansson had not taken Trovald's advice and cooled off over the New Year holiday. If anything, his impatience had increased, and a couple of trying days in the office had done nothing to improve his temper. His irritation mounted when he was phoned by an unknown journalist who wanted to meet him and mentioned that he had been introduced by the manager of Wesyls Handels.

Perhaps it was rash of Johansson to have had a couple of glasses of one of the fierier brands of aquavit before Sven turned up at the bar of the Hotel Amaranten, but he excused himself on the grounds that he had a heavy cold coming on. By the time the reporter put in an appearance, Johansson's tetchiness had turned to something close to truculence.

Sven trotted out the mixture of partial truths and downright fabrications which had been handed to him by Trovald, and Johansson lost what remained of his patience and self-control. If the Swedes were going to be told the truth, they deserved to have it in full and unadulterated.

'And you mean to say you didn't spot that Trovald is a member of SÄPO and that he was feeding you with the version they want to see in print!' he exploded. 'Listen, my young, green friend, I shall give you the real story. I was the one who first suggested that the Iraqis were behind the killing of Palme ...' He went on to recount his conversation with Trovald in the Grand Hotel on the day of the funeral. 'Neither Holmér nor SÄPO had the faintest idea of what the Iraqis were up to, but afterwards Trovald was able to persuade his bosses that I was on the right track, and they decided to follow up my theory.'

Two whiskies later, Sven had the low-down on the intercepted message from Baghdad to the Iraqi Embassy and the hope of enticing an Iraqi minister or senior official to defect by the prospect of the 50 million kronor reward which was dangled before them.

Back in his own office, Sven Beckman was in a thoughtful mood. Before discussing with Ruth what might be the contents of her proposed book, he carefully went through the archives and collected a veritable mountain of material from official reports and accounts at the time of the Palme murder and the subsequent investigation. Then he went home and spoke to Ruth.

As for Johansson, when he recovered next day from the sort of hangover which should not be meted out to right-minded civil servants who have suffered the pangs of a social conscience, he was not quite sure that he had acted altogether judiciously in letting Trovald's slippery cat out of the SÄPO bag, but he felt no regret.

'You know you've always been casting about for a good subject for a book,' Sven said to Ruth. 'Well, listen to this.' He recounted his conversation with Birger Trovald and the subsequent revelations of Erik Johansson. Then he reminded her of her own fascination with the mystery of the murder which had occurred only a few hours before she had first set foot in Sweden.

'How about it!' he concluded. 'I've got hold of an enormous amount of stuff, which I'll translate for you. And there's this extraordinary account from Trovald's defector, in addition to what Johansson said. Don't you think it would make a great book?'

Ruth spent some days going over the material with Sven, who had claimed several days' leave due to him from the paper. She sketched out the plan of a book and then got down to work.

She gazed hopefully at the sheet of snowy white paper before her as if, by magic, words would appear on it. The incredible things she had heard from Sven, a careful sifting of what he had learned from Trovald, amended, corrected and amplified by Erik Johansson, were the stuff from which a really gripping book could be constructed. But how to start and what to call it? *Murder Most Foul* she rejected. Too vague and too much like a title for pure fiction, a crime thriller. *The Killing of Olof Palme*? Factual, but dull. Why not *Death of a Statesman*? It had the right ring to it, and if it evoked Arthur Miller, there was no harm in that. With growing confidence, she began to write.

'The setting sun over Baghdad dyed the wisps of cloud the colour of blood.'

10

Aftermath – Two Ghosts and a Hostage

At about the same time as Ruth Freeman was getting down to the writing of her book, Fahdel Barrak was preparing a less extensive literary offering, a confidential memorandum for the President of the state and the members of the Revolutionary Council. It was a masterpiece of self-justification.

The first section dealt with the situation in Iran. Barrak had his own men in Teheran, some of them occupying important and influential posts. There were even a few disaffected army officers who were hoping for a restoration of the monarchy and were prepared to work with any enemy of the Kohmeini regime. They testified to the war-weariness of the Iranian people and the decline in morale. There followed a brief note on the turn-around in the military situation, with the Iraqi army in the process of driving the Iranians from their last strongholds on Iraqi soil. Next came an analysis of the international scene, with Iran totally isolated. It was particularly satisfying that Iran should be universally branded as a state which supported terrorism.

There followed a report on the specific situation in Sweden. The safety of our party and the state depends on efficient gathering of intelligence and the maintenance of absolute loyalty, the twin objectives of our security forces. Hence the necessity for destroying any defectors, such as the traitor Majed Husain. After the Swedish police offered the colossal reward of 50 million kronor, we redoubled our vigilance, and Swedish diplomats in Baghdad were put under special surveillance. We also imposed tighter controls over our own officers who had access to sensitive material. It is gratifying that there has not been one attempt to collaborate with the Swedes by any of our operatives; nor has there been a single symptom of disloyalty

193

reported. All our officers are completely loyal: those few who were not have been eliminated.

Fahdel Barrak did not think it necessary to recount yet again the rationale which had led to the action against Olof Palme. However, he did remind his readers that, in the event of any unforeseeable deterioration in relations with Sweden, he still had a hostage. Wolfgang Granlund remained in a top-security prison.

Everything had been properly taken care of. A sound policy was producing the desired results. Fahdel Barrak was a very contented man.

At the end of September 1988. Ruth Freeman was in London, seeking a publisher for her book. She was expecting a letter from Sven, but postal deliveries had been disrupted by a strike, so she was relieved when at last there arrived a letter with a Swedish stamp. But when she opened it, she found that it came not from Sven but from Erik Johansson.

Dear Ruth,
It was kind of you to let me see the manuscript of your book, and I trust that you found my few corrections helpful. I believe it to be the most accurate account yet put forward of the murder of Olof Palme and the extraordinary police investigation which followed.

However, what has since come to light is not so much extraordinary as fantastic. When Holmér quit after the fiasco with the Kurds, he was still convinced that his current theory was one hundred per cent correct, just as he had been with his previous theory. Only now he suspected that the Kurds had been put up to murder Palme by the Iranians. So, before he left to take up his post in Vienna, a group was formed to continue his line of investigation, in secret and independently of the police. The discovery of this underground group has led to a first-class scandal in the country, and one of the first results was that the Minister of Justice, Anna Greta Leijon, was obliged to resign after less than 300 days in office. It has been established that she formed the group. How could a Minister of Justice back an unofficial organization in competition with the police to work behind their backs?

The arrest of a policeman at Helsingborg triggered off what has been described as Sweden's Watergate. The man was attempting to smuggle into the country sophisticated bugging-devices, estimated to be worth about £30,000. The importing of such equipment is strictly prohibited and is an offence. The ensuing inquiry found that the policeman was working for this group, whose members included Holmér himself and a publisher, Ebbe Carlsson, who acted as leader or, at any rate, co-ordinator. Carlsson is a controversial figure, a self-proclaimed homosexual, and in my opinion a rather bizarre choice for a mission requiring tact and judgement. At least three policemen seem to have been recruited and several politicians, as well as the ambassador to Paris, Carl Lidbom, who formerly, as Minister without Portfolio, had introduced a welter of bureaucratic legislation. It was known that he had a grudge against SÄPO ever since he reported an attempted break-in at the Paris embassy. The SÄPO investigators reported that the disarray, broken and overturned furniture, was the work of the ambassador himself, 'in his cups'. Isn't that a polite way of saying 'pissed'? It has also been alleged that a Mr Åhmansson was involved. He denies this, but it is affirmed by a public prosecutor. Åhmansson was appointed head of the National Police after Romander retired at the beginning of this year.

Well, a public prosecutor has been appointed, and there is certain to be a case brought against some, possibly all, of the conspirators, but already some interesting facts have emerged, a number of which, my dear Ruth, have a bearing on your book.

First, Holmér convinced Ebbe Carlsson of the existence of a Kurdish plot, and Carlsson told Anna Greta Leijon that SÄPO knew of a threat against the life of Palme and did nothing to counter it. If the minister had given as much time to the responsible police chiefs as she did to Carlsson, she would have been better briefed and would have known that the Kurds were preparing for an assassination which took place in Hamburg and had no relevance to Palme or anyone else in Sweden. Carlsson also claimed to have 'information' from a PKK defector, but all this amounted to was an unsubstantiated claim that Iran was in one way or another involved in the killing of Palme. Neither Carlsson nor anyone else has been able to suggest any credible motive for the Iranians to commit an atrocity in a country which both openly and covertly was doing so much to sustain their war effort. A suggestion that Palme was on the point of stopping or interfering with the flow of material to Teheran sounds suspiciously like Iraqi disinformation, since there was absolutely no way he could constitutionally have taken such action and there is not a shred of evidence that he would have wanted to do so. Indeed, quite the contrary. What has emerged from the investigation of the sale of arms by Bofors and other manufacturers shows that Palme was only too aware of the need for them to export if they were to remain viable and that on occasion, notably in the case of India, he used his personal influence to help them to obtain contracts. If anything, his attitude towards the flow of arms and material would have constituted a motive for the Iraqis, not the Iranians.

Holmér was sufficiently obsessed by his ideas of the conspiracy that he went to elaborate lengths and enormous expense to maintain and equip his own bodyguards. It is stated that he spent 3 million kronor on paying them overtime and on such items as guns more powerful than police regulation weapons, and even a brief-case which contained a gun with the trigger mounted in the handle. Now why on earth would the head of the Stockholm Police District need something like that, straight out of a James Bond scenario? He had not been threatened and, indeed, does not appear to have been a logical target, even for the groups which he at one time or another accused.

But Anna Greta Leijon got caught up in this wave of hysteria, and she provided Carlsson with a letter of introduction stating that he was acting on her behalf, and it was this which demonstrated her involvement with the smuggling of illegal equipment into the country. I enclose a copy which I suggest you reproduce in your book, despite its appalling English.

All of this came out during a parliamentary inquiry which was televised live. There was a memorable moment when Carlsson interrupted the vice-chairman of the Constitutional Committee (the parliamentary body which deals with alleged unconstitutional behaviour by ministers) to claim that he knew more about the organization of SÄPO than anyone else present. 'That is precisely what worries me,' replied the vice-chairman. Later, Näss, who had resigned as head of the Counter-Espionage Division and had been appointed head of the

Uppsala Police District, concluded a forceful statement with the words: 'If a foreign power had set out to damage our security system and our counter-espionage forces, I dare to claim that they could not have been more successful than what Carlsson and his associates have achieved.'

Näss was distressed by what he saw as the loss of confidence in the Swedish security forces by our friends in other countries. What worries me is, how can we expect a successful prosecution of the Palme affair when the police and the Government are so clearly at each other's throats and neither party has any confidence in the other, and when the case is entrusted to dilettantes and political appointees?

But let me give you a couple of snippets of information which bear on Iraq. We now know that, on the very last day of his life, Palme received the Iraqi ambassador. It was a private meeting – it had to be, since the normal procedure is for an ambassador to be received by the Head of Protocol, the chief of the Political Department or the secretary of the cabinet of the Minister of Foreign Affairs or, of course, the Minister of Foreign Affairs himself, according to the importance of the subject. No notes were taken, an unusual feature, but it is possible that Palme would have written a report if he had lived. More surprising is that no one else was present throughout the meeting, which lasted no less than two hours. Nothing is known of what was said, or why the meeting even took place, and a two-hour session with any prime minister is exceptional, let alone as busy a man as Palme. Suspicious? Certainly intriguing!

You may wonder why this meeting was not mentioned in the early stages of the investigation. What appears to have happened is that, while Holmér's army of detectives snooped on Palme's known political enemies and enquired into who had checked into all the city's hotels or left cars illegally parked near the exits of Tunnelgatan, quite a time elapsed before they got round to investigating Palme's private life and his own movements on the day of his murder. As you know, a lot of the professional police were very critical of Holmér's methods. They would claim that the Ebbe Carlsson affair had demonstrated just how right they were.

A cynical touch. Claes Palme, Olof's brother, was invited

to lunch by the Iraqi ambassador a little more than a year after the murder. When the Gulf War is over, the ambassador said, a statue of Olof Palme would be erected in Baghdad. He did not give any reason for honouring the man who, as UN mediator, had been attacked as being pro-Iranian.

But no statue will bring Palme back to life, and the killers of him and of that indiscreet defector Majed Husain walk unpunished. But one victim still lives. Wolfgang Granlund has been left to rot inside an Iraqi gaol. Isn't it amazing that American, British and German hostages held by Iran or its allies in Lebanon are the subjects of repeated diplomatic protests, yet the lone Swede seems to have been conveniently forgotten! His 'trial' was a farce: his offence, being in the wrong place at the wrong time. What a contrast with the protests that were repeatedly made by Sweden to the Soviet Government after the arrest and disappearance of Raoul Wallenberg! So Fahdel Barrak hangs on to his hostage. Maybe your book will do something to draw attention to the plight of this man, the third victim.

Erik Johansson

Epilogue

10 November 1988. In the Gulf, the shooting had stopped. After the destruction of one of their air liners by a US warship, the exhausted Iranians had accepted the conditions of the ceasefire and Taha Maroof, Vice President of Iraq, was making a goodwill visit to Stockholm. Another Swede, Jan Eliasson, had been appointed to succeed Palme as UN mediator in the war: the time had come to kiss and make up! The only obstacle to the restoration of friendly relations between our countries, he had been informed by both Prime Minister Carlsson and Foreign Minister Andersson, was the fate of the unfortunate Wolfgang Granlund, still held behind bars in Iraq. Nobody mentioned Majed Husain. Give us back Granlund and the Majed Husain affair will be buried in the dead files. That was the deal which was struck.

Iraq was the only country to have profited from the murder of Olof Palme. The policy of Fahdel Barrak had proved brilliantly successful. The hostage had served his purpose and was no longer needed. A couple of days later, Wolfgang Granlund was back in Stockholm. And not only had the killing of Majed Husain been conveniently consigned to oblivion. So also, in effect, had that of Olof Palme. The murder of Husain had created a problem: that of Olof Palme had wiped the slate clean.

Anyone who would make a pilgrimage today to the spot where Olof Palme was gunned down will look in vain for the street named, Tunnelgatan. The road has been renamed. Now it is known as Olof Palmes Gata, and on the spot where he fell a sad little heap of flowers which are constantly renewed can still usually be seen. There is a great deal of talk of some more lasting tribute: doubtless, in time to come, other, more dignified monuments will be erected to the memory of Olof Palme.

Index

(Names are listed in Swedish alphabetical order. After Z comes Å, Ä, Ö.)